OCR **Psychology**
for GCSE

Psychology First

THIRD EDITION

Barbara Woods
Karon Oliver and Phil Banyard

HODDER
EDUCATION
HACHETTE UK COMPANY

Orders: please contact Bookpoint Ltd, 130 Milton Park, Abingdon, Oxon OX14 4SB. Telephone: (44) 01235 827720. Fax: (44) 01235 400454. Lines are open from 9.00 – 5.00, Monday to Saturday, with a 24-hour message answering service. You can also order through our website www.hoddereducation.co.uk

If you have any comments to make about this, or any of our other titles, please send them to educationenquiries@hodder.co.uk

British Library Cataloguing in Publication Data
A catalogue record for this title is available from the British Library

ISBN: 978 0 340 98532 8

First Edition Published 2001
Second Edition Published 2006
This Edition Published 2009
Impression number   10 9   8 7 6 5 4 3 2 1
Year   2012, 2011, 2010, 2009

Hachette UK's policy is to use papers that are natural, renewable and recyclable products and made from wood grown in sustainable forests. The logging and manufacturing processes are expected to conform to the environmental regulations of the country of origin.

Cover photo © Hannes Nimpuno/iStockphoto.com.
Illustrations by Barking Dog Art.
Typeset by Fakenham Photosetting Ltd, Fakenham, Norfolk.
Printed in Italy for Hodder Education, an Hachette UK Company, 338 Euston Road, London NW1 3BH

CONTENTS

INTRODUCTION

By picking up this book, you will have made the decision to start exploring one of the most amazing subjects that you will ever encounter. Psychology is about you – because it studies the way that you and other humans (and sometimes other species) think, communicate, remember and behave, how they interact with each other, how they develop and mature, how they are alike and how they are different.

This subject will have a tremendous relevance to all aspects of your life, not only now but also in the future. Personally, for me, psychology has inspired me, has made me want to know and understand more, has never bored me and has led me into a fascinating career. I am now in the fortunate position of being able to apply the knowledge I have, working as an educational psychologist specialising in children's behaviour.

You will probably be reading this particular book because you are about to study a GCSE in the subject (although it is also relevant to other readers with just a general interest). The aim of the syllabus is to help you, the student, have a greater understanding about psychology, about the nature of research and to help you to critically evaluate information you are given, for example from newspapers or the television, rather than just accepting what you are told. In fact, in many ways, developing these skills will make you challenge *far more* of the information you receive and help you to think and reflect on common misconceptions. You will also develop an awareness of why psychology matters and how the findings from psychological research influence the way that we live and work alongside our fellow human beings. You will become aware of ethical issues in research carried out on humans and gain an understanding of how psychology contributes to our understanding of individual, social and cultural diversity.

The design of the OCR GCSE syllabus:
The syllabus is divided into five topics which cover the different approaches to psychology.

1 The Biological approach looks at humans as biological creatures. It considers how our biological make-up influences our behaviour.
2 The Cognitive approach focuses on what we remember, how we interpret what we see and how we think.
3 The Developmental approach considers the way that we grow and develop in our thinking and reasoning and how we learn.
4 The Social approach considers humans as social beings, focusing on the impact of others on our behaviour and how we interpret the behaviour of others.
5 The Individual Differences approach looks at how we are each unique and actually questions whether we should compare ourselves to each other.

When psychologists develop theories about how humans (and animals) interact, behave, think and respond, they have to test their theories by undertaking research. In Chapters 6 and 7, you can read all about the way that this research is carried out. It is not easy to research people in the same way as it is to research inanimate objects and this is why you will need to understand the weaknesses of many of the techniques used. This understanding is also important because the syllabus requires you to be able to understand and carry out your own research using either an experiment, a questionnaire, an interview or an observation.

The aims of the GCSE specification are to enable you to:

1 Engage in the process of psychological enquiry in order to develop as effective and independent learners and as critical and reflective thinkers with enquiring minds.

   In order to do this, you will need to learn to seriously think about and evaluate past research. You will then be able to use this knowledge to reflect on all statistical information and evidence that you are given in all areas of your life. You will learn to ask questions and to look beyond the surface, especially when you hear things reported in the media.

2 Develop an awareness of why psychology matters.

   Psychology matters because psychology is all around us, in everything we do and in all that we experience. You will probably have noticed how psychologists are called upon for their opinion in most areas of life, from child development to schooling, to work, to health, to environmental design, to marketing, to critical incidents and so on.

3 Acquire knowledge and understanding of how psychology works and its essential role in society.

   When learning about the different approaches in psychology, you will also be able to make the links between each particular topic. At the end of every chapter is a section you will read about how research into psychology is actually used in practical areas of our lives.

4 Develop an understanding of the relationship between psychology and social, cultural, scientific and contemporary issues and the impact of psychology on everyday life.

   In the social psychology chapter in particular, you will find that the issues discussed relate to a large extent to our everyday lives.

5 Develop an understanding of ethical issues in psychology.

   In order to protect ourselves and others from misguided research which could damage our well being, we will consider ethical guidelines which are intended to protect participants from experiencing any long-term difficulties.

6 Develop an understanding of the contribution of psychology to individual, social and cultural diversity.

   You will be able to see how psychology has identified our similarities and differences and has helped to explain how these come about.

7 Develop a critical approach to scientific evidence and methods.

   You will learn to question research evidence rather than accepting everything you are told at face value. Developing evaluative skills will stand you in good stead in all areas of your life.

As a word of caution, it is likely, once you mention to others that you are studying psychology, that they will immediately think that you can analyse them and will know what they are thinking. Well, take it from me, you will no more be able to do this with 100% accuracy at the end of your studies than you will at the begininning. What you will be able to do, though, is use your knowledge to make an informed 'guestimation' (a cross between an informed guess and an estimation based on what you would expect from people in a similar situation)! Remember, psychology is not so much about analysing but is more about understanding and predicting based on sound research.

The design of the book:
The book is divided into six chapters. The first five chapters focus on the different approaches to psychology whilst the final chapter focuses on research. In order to explain how the book relates to the OCR GCSE syllabus, it will help you to look at the design of the syllabus and understand how it is divided into three units:

The following is taken directly from the syllabus (p. 6):

2.1   GCSE Units

Unit B541: Studies and Applications in Psychology 1	
Biological Psychology:	• Sex and gender
Cognitive Psychology:	• Memory
Developmental Psychology:	• Attachment
Social Psychology:	• Obedience
Individual Differences:	• Atypical behaviour

Unit B542: *Studies and Applications in Psychology 2*	
Biological Psychology:	• Criminal behaviour
Cognitive Psychology:	• Perception
Developmental Psychology:	• Cognitive development
Social Psychology:	• Non-verbal communication
Individual Differences:	• The self

Unit B543: *Research in Psychology*

Planning research

Doing research

Analysing research

Planning an investigation

This book has put the two related sections together so, for example, the two biological sections are contained in the first chapter covering sex and gender and criminal behaviour. The second chapter covers cognitive psychology (memory and perception). The third chapter focuses on developmental psychology (attachment and cognitive development). The fourth chapter focuses on social psychology (obedience and non-verbal communication) and the fifth chapter on individual differences (atypical behaviour and the self).

The last chapter links to the final Unit B543 by first of all giving you an introduction to how psychological research is conducted and then by describing how to plan, undertake and analyse research.

In order to help you to see how each section relates to the syllabus, I have included the wording of the syllabus at the beginning of each new section which can be found in a text box explaining 'Candidates should be able to ...'

Key terms are given in bold type and explained in the Glossary.

Core Studies:
Each chapter contains two pieces of actual psychological research which are taken from each of the different approaches to psychology. Sometimes research papers are quite difficult to understand and contain a great deal of statistical information, so what I have tried to do is to keep all the relevant information but to simplify the way the research is written. *On some occasions I have included, within the studies, some text in italics which should help to explain what the authors meant*.

Although the studies are quite long, you *will not* need to know every detail but to have a general understanding of what the studies were about. It will be useful for you to focus on the following areas:

- The method – was it an experiment or a case study or an observation?
- Participants – who were they, how were they selected and was it a small or large sample?
- Procedure – what did the participants actually do? For example, did they complete a questionnaire or were they observed?

- Results – what did the results show (generally)?
- Conclusions – what does the result mean?
- Strengths and weaknesses in design or methodology.
- Any applications the research might have to everyday life

If you come across references in the studies, these are mentioned by the authors and will therefore not appear in the bibliography at the back of the book.

You will find that by going to the OCR website and looking at the OCR GCSE syllabus, you can get more detailed information about the examination, coursework, ethical issues, teacher training and further reading. The OCR website is www.ocr.org.uk.

Enjoy!
Karon Oliver

PREFACE

This book, written specifically for the new OCR GSCE syllabus, is one of a series of new texts being published by Hodder Headline. It has been my great pleasure to collaborate with Barbara Woods, the original author of Psychology First, and Phil Banyard, a very experienced teacher and well-known author, in the writing of this text.

PICTURE CREDITS

Biological psychology

Biological psychology is concerned with the role that biology plays in our behaviour and experience. Biological psychology looks at people as if they are biological machines. This might sound like a strange idea, but when you think about it you can see that our biology affects our behaviour and experience. On a simple level we know that the things we eat and drink, such as coffee or alcohol, will affect the way we see the world and the way we behave. Also, it has been observed for a long time that damage to the brain and nervous system can have an effect on behaviour and experience. So the action of chemicals and the structure of the nervous system are the two main themes of biological psychology. However, the question that is most frequently asked is how much our biology makes us what we are, and what other factors intervene to affect our behaviour.

- The first section in this chapter looks at the interaction between biology and psychology by considering sex and gender. The core study relating to this issue is an article reporting the long-term follow-up to a case where a little boy had his penis accidentally cut off when he was a baby and was consequently raised as a little girl.
- The second section looks at the interaction between experience and biology by considering criminal behaviour. The study at the end of the chapter considers whether genetics or environment have a greater impact on criminality.

SEX AND GENDER

OVERVIEW

'Is it a girl or a boy?' is one of the first questions a new parent asks. The answer will affect how the baby is treated and how the child views her/himself. Our society has different expectations of men and women, and the growing child soon learns what they are. But to what extent are these differences due to our biological make-up? This section first considers biological differences between males and females, considers evolutionary change in males and females, and then reviews several explanations for how children come to adopt the attitudes and behaviours that their society considers appropriate to their sex.

KEY CONCEPTS

The OCR examination requires candidates to be able to:

- distinguish between sex and gender
- outline the concepts of masculinity, femininity and androgyny.

DEFINITIONS OF SEX AND GENDER

The words sex and gender are sometimes used as though they mean the same thing, and on other occasions as though they have different meanings. They do have different meanings, as explained below.

- **Sex** refers to the biological aspects of the individual. For example, a child's sex is identified at birth by its genitals.
- **Gender** refers to the psychological and cultural aspects of maleness or femaleness.

Men are considered to be **masculine** if they take on what society considers to be the appropriate gender role. In most cultures, this gender role suggests that men should be strong, bold and fearless – the protector and provider for the family. In the past, men who chose to stay at home and look after children while their wives worked, or who chose professions such as ballet dancing, were not considered to be masculine.

The qualities that are thought to convey **femininity** are more nurturing. In the past, most cultures have focused on gentleness and sensitivity as truly feminine traits, regarding competitiveness and aggression as qualities which would make a woman appear more masculine.

If a person does not appear to be either masculine or feminine and appears to be of an indeterminate gender, we say they are **androgynous**. In fact, some famous performers have taken on an androgynous role, appealing to both men and women. One example was David Bowie, who took the role of 'Ziggy Stardust' in 1972 when he released the album *The Rise and Fall of Ziggy Stardust and the Spiders from Mars*.

CORE THEORY: biological theory

Candidates should be able to:

- outline the role of chromosomes in typical gender development
- outline the role of gonads and hormone production in typical gender development
- describe basic evolutionary sex differences in human behaviour
- explain the criticisms of the biological theory of gender development.

BIOLOGICAL THEORY

The role of chromosomes in typical gender development

When an egg is fertilised, the child's sex is determined by the sperm that fertilises the egg. This is because the man's sperm contains one chromosome, which will either be X or Y, whereas the mother's egg always contains the X chromosome. Therefore, if the man's sperm contains the X chromosome, the baby will then have XX, which will be female. If the sperm contains the Y chromosome the baby will then have XY chromosomes and will be a boy.

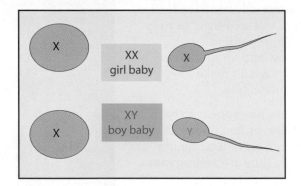

These two chromosomes are needed for the development of the internal and external sex organs. Babies are formed with the *possibility* of being either a girl or a boy as both have two body parts called **gonads**.

The role of gonads in typical gender development

If the fertilising sperm contains the X chromosome, the gonads will develop into ovaries. However, if the sperm contains the Y chromosome, the gonads will develop into testes which start to produce the chemical testosterone – a **hormone**. It is at this point that the genetic influences on sex cease and hormones take over the biological sex determination.

The role of hormones in typical gender development

Until the seventh week of development in the womb, all babies' **genitals** (the external sex organs) look the same. After that time, testosterone is responsible for a change in the external sex organs of boys, as a penis and scrotum develop. The ovaries in the female foetus produce oestrogen and progesterone, which lead to the development of the womb and the vagina. In fact, both sexes produce these hormones, but in different quantities.

External genitalia

If the hormone levels are unusual, this can have a number of repercussions. For example, low levels of testosterone in the womb result in the child appearing to have female external genitals at birth even though the child may have XY chromosomes. Because the genitals are the first indicator of the sex of a newborn child they are going to impact on the subsequent behaviour of the adults who come into contact with the child. Past research has shown that parents interact differently with boys and girls right from the start, with boys being given more intense and varied stimulation than girls. One study looked at adults' responses to a six-month-old boy baby, dressed in identical outfits, one of which was pink and the other blue. Participants were asked to hand the baby a toy, which could have been either a train (boy's toy), doll (girl's toy) or a fish (neutral). When the baby was dressed in blue, he was given the train significantly more often than the other two toys. Similarly, when he was dressed as a girl, he was given the doll significantly more frequently. These studies indicate how important external genitals are in determining the behaviour of others towards a child.

Puberty

Puberty triggers further changes in hormone levels, with higher levels of oestrogen being produced by the ovaries in girls and testosterone being produced by the testes in boys. These and other hormones have a dramatic effect on both girls and boys, physically (see Table 1.1) and emotionally.

GIRLS		BOYS	
Characteristics	Age of occurrence	Characteristics	Age of occurrence
Breasts grow	8–13 years	Testes and scrotal sac grow	10–13 years
Pubic hair develops	8–14 years	Pubic hair develops	10–15 years
The body grows and becomes more 'curvy' in shape	9½–14½ years	The body grows and becomes more muscular	10½–16 years
Uterus and vagina grow and periods start (menarche)	10–16½ years	Penis grows	11–14½ years
Underarm hair grows	Around two years after pubic hair	Voice changes (larynx grows)	Around the same time as the penis
Oil/sweat glands become more active	Around time of underarm hair	Underarm and facial hair appears	Around two years after pubic hair
		Oil/sweat glands become more active	Around time of underarm hair

Table 1.1 Variations in physical changes at puberty for boys and girls

Source: L. A. Goldstein (1976, in L. Steinberg 1996)

Variations in emotional changes and behaviour at puberty for boys and girls

Girls may experience the following behavioural changes:

● they may sleep more
● they may feel more emotional, moody and sometimes aggressive
● they will be aware of sexual feelings
● some girls experience premenstrual syndrome (PMS) around the time of their periods; the effects of PMS vary from person to person, with symptoms as varied as headaches, back pain, irritability, sadness, bloating and breast tenderness.

Boys may experience the following behavioural changes:

● they may sleep more
● they may feel more moody and more aggressive
● they may become more competitive
● they may become more clumsy
● they may think and fantasise about sex
● they may have wet dreams (when they ejaculate in their sleep).

Hormone imbalances

Hormone imbalances in growing children can affect the development of both boys and girls. As we have seen, testosterone is responsible for a number of changes in the bodies of males, including an increase in hair growth, a deepening of the voice, and increased muscle and aggressive behaviour. Therefore women who have higher than normal levels of testosterone will become more masculine in their appearance and behaviour. This can be caused by disorders of the **endocrine system** or it may be due to choice for female bodybuilders, who use anabolic steroids (synthetic versions of the male sex hormone testosterone).

Men who have low levels of testosterone will experience loss of muscle and lack of strength, low sex drive, tiredness and depression. If their levels of oestrogen increase to be higher than normal (remember, both men and women produce both hormones but in differing quantities), they may even exhibit secondary female sex characteristics such as the development of breasts and a reduction in facial hair.

Basic evolutionary sex differences in human behaviour

If biological appearance was the only factor that determined the differences between men and women, then the roles that men and women take would have been consistent over time. However, evolutionary theorists argue that gender roles have gradually evolved over time in response to the changes in our environment.

When we lived as hunter-gatherers and food was sparse, males were required to use their physical strength to go and hunt for food while women stayed at home and looked after the children. Of course, we can't know this for sure because we have no direct evidence of how Stone Age people lived. This story of how these people behaved is our best guess, based on our understanding of evolution and our observations of behaviour today.

As we have already seen, hormones affect strength, and women are generally smaller and physically weaker than men, so these roles would make the most sense. Brain areas may also have adapted to enable each sex to carry out their roles. Men developed superior navigation skills, which would have made them more effective hunters. Women, on the other hand, have a preference for landmarks, which would help them to gather food closer to home and, at the same time, reduce their chances of encountering danger (D.C. Geary 1998).

Women's biological role of child bearing requires that they remain safe, and away from the dangers and opportunities that the males faced in order to protect their unborn child. Perhaps morning sickness, which prevents women from wanting some more adventurous foods or foods with a strong taste, may have been a way of stopping the developing foetus from being damaged by potentially harmful foodstuffs.

In evolutionary terms, even women's better verbal skills would make sense because while strong men could pit their strength against others in order to compete or protect, women would have to use language as a way of defending themselves – through arguments, persuasion and manipulation.

Perhaps one of the most liberating aspects for women was the development of effective contraception in the 1960s. This resulted in them having the choice as to whether or not to have children. Once they were in a position to make choices, the need for monogamous relationships and marriage diminished. As a result, family dynamics have changed, with higher levels of divorce and more 'reconstituted' families being formed.

Today women have the potential to be independent, with their own careers and their own houses. A great part of this is to do with changes in the structure of society, the availability of education to a higher level for both sexes and the development of information technology, which gives both men and women more access to information than ever before. Flexibility of working, working at home and increased childcare availability have released women from the role of primary caregiver. Men are no longer seen as strange if they choose to participate fully in child rearing, and **house husbands** are not uncommon. Laws preventing sex discrimination have reduced the differences between the sexes still further.

Where once the physically strong and masculine man was seen as the ideal mate, who would be able to provide resources for his family and protect them, women today look for different things in a husband. Men no longer have to be physically powerful because power can also come from money, knowledge and economic status. How often have you seen a very beautiful young woman on the arm of a much older but very rich man? Women also want men who are nurturing and caring, and who are willing to share the child rearing as many of them have their own careers. The advent of the 'new man' reflected these changes, with many men becoming less **'macho'** and more sensitive to the needs of their partners and children.

What is clear in our society is that men and women do not have clearly defined roles, and this provides a problem for simple evolutionary theories. The behaviour of most animals is clearly defined and we can predict how most males and females will behave. This is not the case with human beings and you will come across men who have a number of characteristics that are often regarded as feminine, such as empathy, and some women who have characteristics that are often regarded as masculine, such as competitiveness. How we behave as men and women is partly a matter of choice, though it is clear that our biology still has a big part to play, as we will see below.

Criticisms of the biological theory of gender development

- If our biological sex was the only factor in gender development, male and female behaviour would remain constant over time, whereas gender roles have changed dramatically.
- Males and females behave very differently in different cultures, whereas if biology was the only factor in gender development, they would all behave in the same way.

- Biological theory does not take into account the fact that children observe the behaviour of others and will copy them. Perhaps they develop their gender-related behaviour from watching others (this is known as social learning theory and is discussed in more detail below, page 28).
- If biological differences were all that mattered, why do transvestites find that dressing in the other gender's clothes makes them feel more comfortable? If the issue was purely biological, they would only feel comfortable with gender reassignment surgery rather than the external apparel of the other sex.

CORE THEORY: psychoanalytic theory

Candidates should be able to:

- consider psychoanalytic theory as an alternative theory, with specific reference to the role of the Oedipus/Electra complex in gender development.

PSYCHOANALYTIC THEORY AND GENDER ROLES

An alternative theory that can be used to explain gender development is based on the work of Sigmund Freud. According to Freud's psychoanalytic theory, instinctive drives underlie human behaviour. The way we cope with one of these drives – the libido, or life instinct – is what underpins the development of our gender role. Freud's theory is very long and can sometimes appear quite strange, especially when it is summarised in textbooks. One main idea of the theory is that children have a range of feelings that they find hard to make sense of. The process of making sense of these feelings is what changes us from children to adults. In brief, Freud proposed the following ideas.

- **At about four years of age** the child's libido creates a desire for the opposite-sex parent. However, the child also fears that the same-sex parent will be very angry when this desire is discovered. This creates anxiety in the child, because of his conflicting emotions of desire and fear, but the child is not aware of these feelings because they are in his unconscious.
- **A boy experiences the Oedipus conflict** because of his desire for his mother and fear that his father will castrate him. To resolve this conflict (to reduce anxiety), the boy identifies with his father – he adopts his father's behaviours, speech and attitudes. The boy feels that his father is less likely to harm him, and behaving like his

father will bring the boy closer to his mother. So the boy internalises male characteristics through **identification** with his father and starts to behave as a male.

- **A girl experiences the Electra conflict**: she has unconscious longings for her father and fears loss of her mother's love. Because she thinks she has already been castrated by her mother, she is not so fearful of her as the boy is of his father. Her **identification** with her mother, in order to reduce the conflict, is therefore less strong than that of the boy with his father. Nevertheless, she adopts the characteristics of her mother and so her gender role develops.

Evaluation of the psychoanalytic explanation

Although psychoanalytic theory has had a huge impact on ideas in the wider world as well as in psychology, it is difficult to gain evidence to support or to disprove it. This is in part because it is very difficult to measure and test our instinctive drives. Another factor is that because our drives and the causes of our anxiety are in the **unconscious**, they are inaccessible for observing or testing.

However, there are some criticisms of Freud's explanation for gender role development. As an example, according to this explanation, children raised in one-parent families should have a poorly developed gender role (because they do not have a parent of each sex, or there is only a same-sex parent). Research indicates that this is not the case, and that these children develop gender roles as successfully as those raised by two parents.

In summary, sex and gender are very important concepts for us as individuals and also for our society. We still make a lot of judgements about what a person can do on the basis of what sex they are. Although we are assigned to our sex role at birth we can play out our gender role with a lot of variations. The question that arises is how much of our behaviour is under biological control and how much can we choose to change? Freud suggested that 'biology is destiny', which means that if you are born with male genitals then you can only be male. But how true is this? The tragic case of David Reimer, which is the core study for this section, gives us further evidence to help us with this question.

 CORE STUDY: Diamond and Sigmundson (1997)

Diamond, M. and Sigmundson, H.K. (1997) Sex reassignment at birth: long-term review and clinical implications. Archives of Paediatrics and Adolescent Medicine, 151, pp. 298–304.

Candidates should be able to:

- describe Diamond and Sigmundson's case study of the castrated twin boy raised as a girl

- outline the limitations of Diamond and Sigmundson's study.

Background

If a child is born with external genitalia that are not obviously male or female, or if their genitalia are seriously damaged in some way, physicians will have to make the decision as to whether the child should be given either a male or female form. In the past, the decision has usually been taken to make the child physically look like a girl if the penis is extremely small and unlikely to function sexually when the child is an adult, because of the possible **psychosexual** consequences a non-functioning penis would cause.

The reason for this decision is because doctors hold the following beliefs:

- that babies are psychosexually neutral at birth (that gender is based on upbringing)
- that healthy psychosexual development depends on the genitals looking 'normal'.

These beliefs are based on the work of John Money and colleagues (Money 1961, 1963; Money and Anke A. Ehrhardt 1972; Money *et al*. 1955).

Diamond and Sigmundson's case study focused on David Reimer. In texts he is commonly given the pseudonym John because his true identity was unknown for more than 20 years. During those 20 years the case was held up as evidence that gender is determined by socialisation and not biology. John was one of a pair of normal XY twins, but at eight months of age he had his penis accidentally burned during an operation that aimed to allow him to pass urine more easily.

It is known that the family were unsure as to how best to deal with this situation, but one evening saw a TV show featuring psychologist John Money. The family made contact with Money, who convinced them to have surgery on John that would make him appear like a girl and to bring him up as a girl.

Money reported the case in 1975. He suggested that John and his family adjusted well to his life as Joan, and that this was evidence that gender identity is not biological but that the 'gender identity gate' is open for at least a year after birth. It was also thought to provide further support for the fact that gender should be based on anatomy, not chromosomes. However, nobody was able to verify this as Money restricted access to the boy and his family. This remained the case until the biologist Milton Diamond was finally introduced to David Reimer ('John'), who was by then an adult and living as a man.

The article

Sigmundson was head of the psychiatric management team in the area where John's family lived, and he kept supervisory control over the case. Diamond, who was an authority on matters of sexuality, had taken a keen interest in the case since it was first made public by Money.

This article challenges the original beliefs that were proposed by Money *et al.* (1955), and was based on information from the following sources:

- a review of the original medical notes and therapists' impressions

- contemporary interviews with John, his mother and his wife.

The aim of the research was to challenge the two medically held claims (postulates), noted above.

Postulate 1: individuals are psychosexually neutral at birth

John/Joan's mother provided the following information:

- Joan was often more boisterous than her twin brother, enjoying rough-and-tumble play. She would get involved in fights.

- She would ignore the girls' toys she was given and would play with her brother's toys, or gadgets and tools.

- She disliked dresses and would rather dress up in men's clothing.

- She would mimic her father rather than her mother, such as pretending to shave rather than apply lipstick.

- Joan was good-looking but when she started to move or talk it was obvious that she was a boy.

John provided the following information:

> There were little things from early on. I began to see how different I felt and was, from what I was supposed to be. But I didn't know what it meant. I thought I was a freak or something . . . I looked at myself and said I don't like this type of clothing, I don't like the types of toys I was always being given. I like hanging around with the guys and climbing trees and stuff like that and girls don't like any of that stuff. I looked in the mirror and [saw] my shoulders [were] so wide, I mean there [was] nothing feminine about me. I [was] skinny, but other than that, nothing. But that [was] how I figured it out. [I figured I was a guy] but I didn't want to admit it. I figured I didn't want to wind up opening a can of worms. (quoted in Diamond and Sigmundson 1997, p. 302)

John's realisation that he was not a girl happened between the ages of nine and eleven years. It caused him a great deal of distress and, as a result, he considered suicide. He had no friends and was teased about his looks, and called a 'caveman' and a 'gorilla', which resulted in him having a fight with one particular girl. Consequently he was expelled from school.

Despite not having a penis, John often tried to stand to urinate, which caused a mess as it was difficult for him to direct the urine stream.

Doctors gave John the hormone oestrogen at the age of 12 (puberty) which was to help him develop breasts. He often threw the tablets away as he did not want to develop breasts and he refused to wear a bra. His feelings of maleness were too strong.

John finally admitted to his doctor that *he knew* and had known for a long time that he was a boy and started to live as a male from age 14. Following some persuasion, his father finally told him about the unfortunate accident when he was a baby. Finally, doctors agreed to support his return to being a male; he was given male hormones and had a mastectomy (removal of breasts) at age 14, and surgery to reconstruct a penis at ages 15 and 16.

John had no interest in boys but had his first sexual relationship with a girl when he was 18 years old. At the age of 25 he met and married a woman who was older than him, and adopted her children. He explained that, once he was a male, he felt that his attitudes, behaviour and body were at last in harmony.

Postulate 2: healthy psychosexual development is intimately related to the appearance of the genitals

If healthy psychosexual development was related to the appearance of one's genitals, then John should have been happy to be a girl as that is what he looked like – but he never felt happy as a girl. He believed the physicians were more concerned with the appearance of his genitals than his feelings. He hated being examined on hospital visits and, when he was asked what he thought of his genitals, he said he had nothing to compare with except his brother (they had been made to inspect each other's 'bits' by the clinicians at Johns Hopkins Hospital, which John found a very negative experience).

Psychometric tests were used to investigate **gender identity**, and John's results were more typical of a boy than a girl. He was given **psychotherapy** to support him to develop a female identity but he still refused to live as a girl, dressing in jeans and shirts, which were neither masculine nor feminine. He also had dreams about being a boy and wanted to be a mechanic.

John thought that others were small-minded if they believed his personality was linked to whether or not he had a penis. His doctor had told him that, if he pursued his desire to be a boy,

> it's gonna be tough, you're going to be picked on, you're gonna be very alone, you're not gonna find anybody [unless you have vaginal surgery and live as a female]. And I thought to myself, you know I wasn't very old at the time, but it dawned on me that these people gotta be pretty shallow if that's the only thing they think I've got going for me; that the only reason why people get married and have children and have a productive life is because of what they have between their legs … If that's all they think of me, that they justify my worth by what I have

between my legs, then I gotta be a complete loser. (quoted in Diamond and Sigmundson 1997, p. 302)

Although he was still bitter about his experience, John lived successfully as 'a mature and forward-looking man with a keen sense of humor and balance' for many years.

A book about David Reimer's life (Colapinto 2004) gives a much fuller account of the case. The book reports that Reimer could never forget his nightmare childhood and sometimes hinted that he was living on borrowed time. And so he was. In 2002, Reimer's twin brother Brian took his own life with an overdose of antidepressants and David's life became more troubled after this. During the following two years he was made redundant, and his explosive anger and periods of depression created tensions in his marriage. On 4 May 2004 he took his own life.

Comment

The clinical notes and John's memories suggest that he never fully accepted that he was a girl, and it was only when doctors realised the psychological damage this was causing him that they too changed their thinking.

John's parents also found the sex reassignment very difficult and his mother had psychiatric treatment to help manage her feelings. His parents would have been happier dealing with John than Joan, and coping with the effects of his accident, rather than the sex reassignment, which made it necessary for them to lie to their own son about who he was.

The authors explain that this case, together with a number of other similar cases, provides overwhelming evidence that normal humans are not psychosexually neutral at birth but are **predisposed** to interact with their environment in either a male or female way.

Conclusions

The authors conclude that this case provides evidence to refute the original beliefs and suggest that:

- babies are *not* psychosexually neutral at birth and that gender is based more on biology than upbringing

- healthy psychosexual development does *not* depend on the appearance of a person's genitals but is more dependent on biological gender assignation.

The authors suggest that parents and children should be given long-term counselling rather than immediate surgery and sexual reassignment in order to deal with any physical deficit. They point out that teenagers, with the appropriate support, should be able to manage these difficulties as well as they manage other severe disabilities.

Limitations of the study

This study was a case study, only investigating the case of one individual. As with all case studies, this individual may not be representative of other individuals who may have responded very differently (this is something we look at in Chapter 6, page 247).

Because Sigmundson worked as head of the psychiatric management team keeping supervisory control over John's case, he would have been very involved in the decisions that were taken to manage John. He was unlikely to be objective in his descriptions as he was too close to the case to remain unbiased.

Much of the evidence was retrospective, with the researchers looking back over old information, which may have been misinterpreted or some aspects might have been missing.

The researchers interviewed John and his family, asking them to recall things that had happened in the past, which may not have been accurately remembered.

The conclusions from the study, that John was finally correctly gender reassigned and therefore fine were actually quite premature as John eventually committed suicide.

APPLICATION OF RESEARCH INTO SEX AND GENDER: equal opportunities for the sexes

Candidates should be able to:
- explain how psychological research relates to equal opportunities for the sexes, e.g. sex typing in education, gender roles at work, natural differences in choice of leisure activities.

EQUAL OPPORTUNITIES FOR THE SEXES

As we have seen, psychological research has shown that both biological factors and upbringing impact on the development of the sexes. We have also discussed how the gender roles of males and females have become less differentiated over time with the changes in law and work. Despite these changes, women still bear children and men still generally have greater physical strength than women. However, males and females have a choice as to the direction they wish to take as they mature, with girls often choosing what were, historically, male-orientated careers. Despite these changes, sex typing still exists to a certain extent in education, work and choice of leisure pursuits.

Sex typing in education

In past decades, schools frequently channelled girls towards what were considered gender-appropriate subjects, which in turn fed into specific careers. For example, girls were encouraged to pursue literature and the arts, or subjects such as childcare, domestic science (cookery), textiles and secretarial courses, while boys were encouraged to pursue either science, maths, technological subjects or vocational training. Girls who sought alternatives were seen as quite unusual and were often persuaded away from their interests. Often, single-sex schools did not provide girls with broad opportunities, seeing them as inappropriate (or pointless).

Women now have *equal* access to education at every level, and are achieving better grades than boys at primary, secondary and higher educational levels (Department for Children, Schools and Families 2006). However, girls still seem to be faced with complex pressures from both society and culture, which results in these traditional **gender** stereotypes continuing and affecting the choices they make.

A report by the Equal Opportunities Commission (2007) showed that, in schools, as soon as pupils have a choice of what subjects to study, boys typically choose technical and science subjects, and girls pursue caring or arts/humanities/social science subjects. The Department for Education and Science (DfES 2007) reported that this is more evident at A level, with English being the most popular subject choice for girls and maths for boys. The other top subjects for girls were psychology, art and design, sociology and media/film/television studies, while boys chose physics, business studies, geography and physical education.

The Office for National Statistics (2006) discovered that, in further and higher education, the majority of students studying literature and

Training	% male	% female
Early years care and education	3	97
Hairdressing apprentices	9.9	90.1
Construction apprentices	99.2	0.8
Engineering manufacture apprentices	94.8	5.2
Motor industry apprentices	98.6	1.4

Table 1.2 Gender segregation of vocational training

Source: Alison Fuller, Vanessa Beck and Lorna Unwin (2005)

languages are female, while the majority of students studying the sciences, engineering and computing are male. Vocational training is even more highly gender segregated (see Table 1.2).

Gender roles in work

Although girls achieve higher grades than boys at school, the subject choices they make often mean that they do not receive the same financial or social rewards as boys. In fact, women tend to be concentrated in low-paid, gender-stereotyped and often part-time jobs.

Pregnancy and motherhood also impact on women's careers. When a woman takes maternity leave, she might feel less confident on her return to work as things within the work environment may have changed while she was away. Research indicates that women not only tend to take responsibility for childcare arrangements but also try to juggle their career with running the home, and this may affect their desire for, or chances of, promotion at work.

Employment	% male%	female
Heath and social care	21	79
Childcare workers	02	98
Receptionists	05	95
Cleaners	24	76
Senior police officers	90	10
Judiciary	91	09
Directors and chief executives	83	17
Private-sector managers	70	30

Table 1.3 Gender bias in paid employment

Source: Equal Opportunities Commission (2006)

Leisure activities

Leisure activities for all age groups seem to reflect stereotypical gender roles. Girls tend to choose more passive or domestic activities, such as reading, studying, helping around the home, shopping, visiting relatives or taking part in organised activities. Boys, on the other hand, tend to be involved in more active and aggressive pursuits, such as playing computer games, doing hobbies or participating in sports, and seem to prefer unorganised or unsupervised activities.

Data from the Office for National Statistics, surveying people over the age of 16 in 2006/07, indicate that these gender differences continue into adulthood. Women with children seem to have less time to engage in leisure activities and are more likely to focus their leisure time around the children, taking them to and from activities.

It seems that the most common leisure activity for over eight out of ten men and women is watching television. Spending time with family and friends was the second most popular activity for 82 per of women, compared to 75 per cent of men.

Women enjoy shopping more than men. They also prefer cultural activities such as reading, arts and crafts, while men enjoy more physical activities such as DIY and sport and exercise. Men also enjoy computer games more than women.

With regard to sport, there are again gender-related differences, with swimming and diving being the most popular sporting activity for women, while the second most popular activity was working out in the gym or other fitness activities. Men also enjoy working out in the gym but, compared to women, they prefer more outdoor activities.

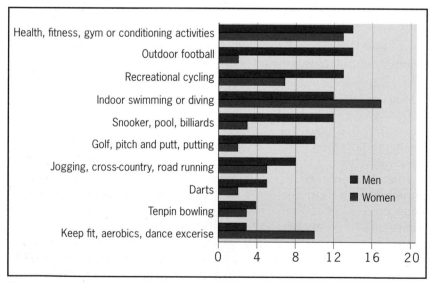

Figure 1.1 Selected sports, games and physical activities among adults, by sex (2006/07, England)
Source: Office for National Statistics (2006/07)

UNIT
B542

CRIMINAL BEHAVIOUR

OVERVIEW

Reports of criminal behaviour appear in the papers or on television on a daily basis – from the most minor incidents, such as the theft of a garden gnome, to the most horrific crimes such as those perpetrated by serial killers such as Harold Shipman or the so-called 'Yorkshire Ripper', Peter Sutcliffe. The victims' relatives, the police, criminal psychologists, psychiatrists and the judiciary all try to understand the reasons why some people turn to crime. One question they frequently ask is whether people are born criminals or whether their behaviour is the result of their upbringing and experience.

KEY CONCEPTS

Crime, measures of crime, criminal personality
The OCR examination requires candidates to be able to:

* outline the problems of defining and measuring crime
* explain the concept of a criminal personality.

DEFINITIONS OF CRIME

The legal definition of crime is an act that breaks the law of the land. However, what is a crime in one country might be seen differently in another. Not only are there variations in what is considered to be a crime between countries, but also between cultures and religions. It is illegal to commit adultery in Muslim society and this crime is punishable by death, yet it occurs on a daily basis among other sectors of society and people rarely comment. Some cultures say it is illegal for a man to have more than one wife, but in parts of the USA and in some Muslim countries it is common practice to do this.

Not only do criminal acts vary between countries and cultures, they also vary over time and circumstance. We know that it is a crime to kill another human being, so why is it different during times of war?

In the UK, in 1967, homosexuality was legalised between consenting adults over the age of 21 in private. Before that it was considered to be a criminal act and, as such, deserved punishments varying from hanging (twelfth century) to hard labour (Victorian times) to prison sentences. Incest was not regarded as a crime until 1908, although now it fills us with horror.

Crimes also have to show intention, which means that we make a judgement about whether a person knew what they were doing and meant to do it. A person who is mentally ill may commit an unlawful act but may escape punishment because we might judge that they were not fully in control of their behaviour.

The age of criminal responsibility also varies from country to country (see Table 1.4). This suggests that an act carried out by a child could be considered a crime in one country but in another they would be judged to be not responsible for their behaviour. Do children differ in their ability to accept responsibility depending on which country they live in? What happens if they move from one country to another? At what age do you think you were old enough to know right from wrong, and be responsible for your own behaviour? (You are not allowed to answer 'Not yet'!)

Country	Age
Scotland	8
England, Wales and Northern Ireland	10
USA (some states)	6
Canada, the Netherlands	12
France	13
Germany, Austria, Italy, Japan, Russia	14
Scandinavian nations	15
Spain, Portugal	16
Brazil, Peru	18

Table 1.4 Age of criminal responsibility in selected countries

These factors indicate how it is impossible to give an accurate definition of crime because the definitions vary according to the time, place and type of act.

Measures of crime

There are several sources of crime measurement, but they may lack accuracy. Data for crime come mainly from the following sources:

- police records – unlikely to record all crimes in an area because some crimes are not reported, such as petty crimes or rape
- surveys undertaken by government officials or by academics from universities – may not be taken seriously by participants or can be affected by experimenter effects (see Chapter 6, page 280).

What is a criminal personality?

There is no one accepted definition of personality but when referring to someone's personality, we generally mean the characteristics that account for relatively consistent patterns of thought and behaviour. It is also important here to remember that we generally think before we act, so our thoughts must have a strong influence on how we behave.

What gives us our personality? Is it inherited or is it the result of our experiences? Most psychologists believe that personality is an interaction between both, with biological inheritance playing a part in the way that we manage our life chances.

Personality is often assessed using personality tests such as the Eysenck Personality Inventory (EPI), which is a pencil and paper test, requiring participants to answer a series of questions which are then scored.

Criminal personality

What we need to consider is whether there are really people who have a 'criminal personality'. If we accept that the way someone thinks will influence their behaviour, then it is likely that criminals have abnormal or unusual thinking patterns. Beth A. Van Houtte *et al.* (1976) suggested that the basis of criminality is in the way criminals think and make decisions, which are different to non-criminals. They also believe that criminals are irresponsible, impulsive, self-centred, and driven by fear or anger.

Hans J. Eysenck (see Figure 1.2) suggested that people with certain features of personality (which he believed are inherited) are more likely to become involved in antisocial behaviour if they experience a certain type of upbringing.

Eysenck initially suggested that there are two major dimensions of personality: **extraversion/introversion** and **neuroticism** (also known as

Figure 1.2 Hans J. Eysenck

emotional instability))/stability; later he added a third dimension known as **psychoticism**, which was at right angles to the other dimensions on his illustration (see Figure 1.3). The EPI will place us all somewhere on these dimensions and, depending on where we fall, we can identify our likely characteristics.

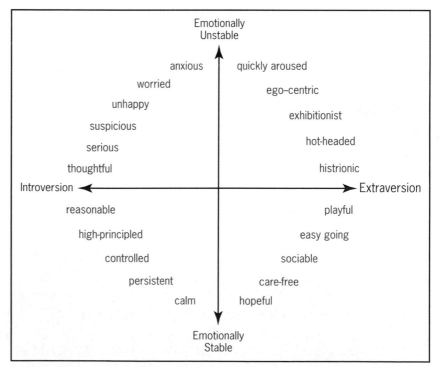

Figure 1.3 The personality traits associated with Eysenck's dimensions

Eysenck believed that the differences between people can be put down to differences in the way their nervous system responds – in particular, the **autonomic nervous system**, which acts as the control system of our bodies, keeping a check on all those things we need to stay alive (like breathing and keeping our hearts beating) but don't need to think about. These levels of arousal correlate with Eysenck's traits of extraversion (under-aroused nervous system) and neuroticism (over-aroused nervous system).

Psychoticism is marked by aggressive, hostile and inconsiderate behaviour. People with low levels of psychoticism are unselfish, warm, and pleasant. Eysenck suggested that the physiological basis for psychoticism is testosterone, with higher levels of psychoticism associated with higher levels of testosterone. Not surprisingly, men score more highly on psychoticism than women.

Eysenck's conclusions were that people who score highly on extraversion, neuroticism and psychoticism are more likely to be associated with violent crime.

It would be really convenient to be able to give someone a personality test and then decide whether they were a criminal or not. However, things are not that easy, and many factors will influence a person's life, including their family and their environment. Most people do something in their lives that is against the law, and some people do it a lot more often than others. The question is whether the people who do it a lot more often are actually a different type of person (a criminal) or just an ordinary person who does criminal things more often.

CORE THEORY: biological theory

Candidates should be able to:

- explain the role of heritability in criminal behaviour

- explain the facial features associated with criminals

- explain the criticisms of the biological theory of criminal behaviour

- consider social learning theory as an alternative theory, with specific reference to vicarious reinforcement of role models in the learning of criminal behaviour

- explain the role of brain dysfunction in criminal behaviour.

BIOLOGICAL THEORY

The role of heritability in criminal behaviour

In the past, researchers looked at the family trees of criminals and, as a result, concluded that criminal tendencies run in families. More recent studies have also shown that a small number of repeat offenders often do come from the same family. Therefore research has tried to identify whether criminality is inherited.

One way to investigate whether *any* traits are inherited is to conduct **twin studies**. This is done by looking at identical (monozygotic, or MZ) twins and comparing them to non-identical (dizygotic, or DZ) twins. MZ twins share the same genetic material, whereas DZ twins share only 50 per cent of their genes. If the MZ twins are more similar than the DZ twins, this would suggest a genetic influence. The degree of similarity between twins is known as the **concordance rate**. If the concordance rate is 100 per cent in MZ twins, this would indicate that the trait is genetic.

Research suggests that there is some degree of genetic link for criminality, but the concordance rate is only 55 per cent for monozygotic twins (Bartol 1999). However, it is very difficult to remove the influence of the twins' life experiences. After all, twins are very likely to have had identical life experiences – especially if they are MZ twins, who even look the same. How do you separate experience from genetics without taking one of the twins out of their environment and giving them a completely different life experience?

In the absence of research on MZ twins reared apart, another way of considering whether criminal behaviour is inherited is to compare adopted children with their non-criminal adoptive parents and their criminal biological parents. The core study at the end of this section by Mednick and colleagues (1984) compares adopted criminals with their biological and adoptive fathers, and concludes that there must be a genetic link as the adopted children are more like their biological parents than their adoptive parents.

The role of brain dysfunction in criminal behaviour

Researchers have considered that criminal behaviour may be the result of brain dysfunction, rather than heritability. This could be caused by brain damage, abnormalities in brain structure or by disturbances in brain chemistry (neurochemicals).

Brain damage

The case of Phineas Gage (1823–60) provided considerable information about the function of the brain. Phineas worked as a railroad construction foreman. He was involved in an accident at work, which drove a large iron rod through his head, entering his

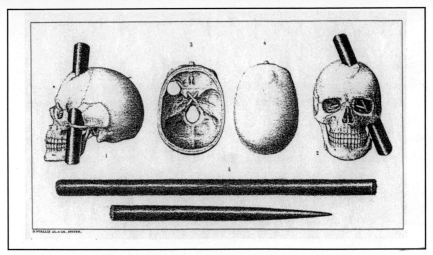

Figure 1.4 This picture shows the entry point into Phineas's skull, just below the left eye

cheek, passing behind his left eye and leaving via the top of his head (as shown in the drawing here). Amazingly, he survived but the rod destroyed a lot of brain tissue in his frontal lobes.

The frontal lobes of the brain are thought to be the emotional control centre and are involved in problem solving, memory, judgement, impulse control, and social and sexual behaviour. Therefore any damage to these lobes is likely to affect a person's emotional and behavioural control. This is what happened to Phineas, who changed from a mild-mannered and considerate man into one who was more challenging, impatient, obstinate and rude.

This case indicates how the effects of brain damage could result in criminal behaviour. After all, impulse control is what prevents us from resisting our less socially acceptable urges, such as taking something we want when it doesn't belong to us, or shouting at our teacher or boss when they annoy us.

Abnormalities in brain structure

Brain damage can be caused by tumours rather than trauma. Charles Whitman, who was a student of architectural engineering at the University of Texas, shot and killed 14 people (including his wife and mother) and wounded a further 31 when he was 25 years old. He bought ammunition on the morning of the murders, took himself to the tallest building so he had a good view of the university campus, and then systematically shot everyone in sight.

Whitman was only stopped when he was shot by police marksmen. His body was sent for post-mortem, where it was discovered that he had a cancerous tumour in the hypothalamus region of the brain. This

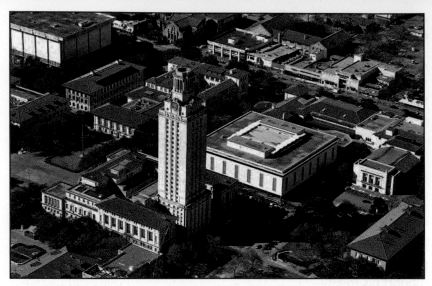

Figure 1.5 The tower at the university where Whitman positioned himself to shoot his victims

may have been pressing on the amygdala, which is linked to a person's mental and emotional state. However, research into Whitman's early years indicated that he may also have been affected by his childhood experiences, his father being very tyrannical and not allowing him to play or socialise with other children.

Facial features associated with criminals

In 1876, Italian criminologist Cesare Lombroso suggested that 40 per cent of criminals were 'born criminals' and it was possible to identify them from their skull and facial features. He collected the physical measurements of criminals and non-criminals using craniometers and calipers, and conducted post-mortem examinations, concluding that criminals differed from non-criminals in their appearance. Through his work, he claimed that criminals had the following physical characteristics:

- a head that was different in size and shape to the heads of those of the same race
- asymmetry of the face
- eye defects or peculiarities
- large jaws and cheekbones
- ears that were either very small or that stood out from the head like the ears of a chimpanzee
- twisted, upturned or flattened nose in thieves
- aquiline or beak-like noses in murderers
- swollen nostrils and a pointed tip to the nose in other criminals
- fleshy, swollen and protruding lips
- cheeks that look like they have pouches in them, like a hamster

- some peculiarities of the palate or a cleft palate
- a chin that was either receding, excessively long or short and flat (as in apes)
- abnormal teeth
- lots of wrinkles
- hair that was more like the hair of the opposite sex.

He also suggested that criminals had excessively long arms. These features, he concluded, suggested that criminals were reverting to a primitive type of man, with physical features similar to those of apes.

Lombroso also tried to identify characteristics of female criminals, but concluded that female criminals were rare and suggested that they had not 'degenerated' in the same way as men because they had 'evolved less than men due to the inactive nature of their lives' (R. Burke 2001).

Despite the interest in Lombroso's suggestions, there is no evidence to support his theory. His criminal sample included a number of people with significant learning difficulties, and we know that a number of

Figure 1.6 This picture, taken from Cesare Lombroso's book, *Criminal Man* (1887), suggests that people can be organised into categories – for example, 'A' are all shoplifters, 'B' are swindlers, 'H' are purse snatchers, 'E' are murderers, and so on

genetic problems can cause both unusual appearance and learning difficulties. Therefore these people may have been involved in criminal activities because of their learning difficulties rather than because they were actually 'born criminals'. A further study, by Charles Goring (1913), compared 3000 convicts to a control sample but found no differences between the two groups.

Criticisms of the biological theory of criminal behaviour

Trying to separate the biological basis of criminal behaviour from the environmental and social effects is extremely difficult. The only way that it might be possible to separate the two is to raise two children from the same family in social isolation and then look at their behaviour as adults. Obviously, this is not possible and so we are left with the question as to whether biological explanations are sufficient to understand criminal behaviour.

Strengths

Some physical conditions seem to suggest that criminal behaviour is more likely and therefore these people could be more closely monitored for signs of criminal behaviour in the future.

Identifying unusual levels of brain chemicals means that they can be treated with medication. This can help manage behaviour, which may, in turn, prevent the person from becoming involved in criminal activities.

Weaknesses

It is extremely difficult to separate some of the biological causes of crime from environmental and life experiences. It can never be proved that criminal behaviour is inherited because criminal families also share a common environment and life experiences.

This is especially likely when we consider MZ twins, who look alike and may therefore generate more similar social responses from others than do DZ twins. Not only do they share the same genes, they may also share an almost identical social environment. Most studies into criminal behaviour have only a very small sample size because of the problems involved in obtaining access to criminal twins. There are also many people who have the biological factors that may predispose them to criminal behaviour but who, nevertheless, never become criminals.

SOCIAL LEARNING THEORY

Psychologists have always been interested in how people learn. Research focusing on animals has shown that they learn specific behaviours if they receive some sort of reward. For example, if we want to teach a dog to sit, we can reward it by offering it a doggie choc. It will soon learn that the outcome of sitting down in front of its owner is a reward. This is known as **operant conditioning** and involves giving the dog some kind of **reinforcement** or reward in order to convince it that the behaviour is worth repeating. It is similar with people – we are more likely to learn something if we see it as being worthwhile (we get some sort of reward for learning). Would you be happy to do lots of examinations if they did not lead to some sort of qualification? Would you work if you weren't paid?

Social learning theory is an alternative learning theory and proposes that we learn not simply by reinforcement, but also by observing other people and imitating their behaviour, which is why it is also called observational learning. Albert Bandura's studies of aggression form the basis for the principles of social learning, as you can see below.

Social learning theory and criminal behaviour

We frequently watch other people, and children in particular observe others a great deal of the time. When they are observing others, they notice what they do and how they do it, what they say and how they say it. They also observe the consequences of other people's behaviour, and this may affect whether they imitate it or not.

Models

In social learning theory, anyone whose behaviour is observed is called a model. You have probably heard people say 'He's not a good role model' when talking about someone whose behaviour is unacceptable. The type of people who are more likely to be models are those who are:

- **similar** – such as someone of the same sex, same age, same family or with the same interests
- **powerful** – such as a relative, teacher, pop star, sports star, cartoon hero or heroine
- **caring** – such as a parent or teacher
- **reinforced** – if the child sees that the model's behaviour leads to pleasant consequences (such as gaining approval), they are more likely to copy it.

Imitation and reinforcement

If the observer imitates the behaviour, we know that the behaviour has been learned. For example, a boy might punch his teddy bear in the same way as the hero in a cartoon punched another character. The child may say the same things or imitate the noises that accompanied the punch. If other characters in the cartoon showed admiration for this action, the child is even more likely to copy the hero's behaviour. This would be an example of **vicarious reinforcement** whereby the observer learns that the behaviour is worth imitating.

However, you can see from Bandura's research (described below) that, even though the behaviour has been learned, it is not necessarily performed.

The individual is more likely to perform the behaviour again if they are rewarded or reinforced for doing so. If the boy punches like the cartoon character and wins admiration from his friends, this reinforcement means that he is likely to continue. However, he is less likely to do it at home if his parents disapprove of his behaviour, as their disapproval acts as punishment. So the individual learns to behave in different ways, depending on the circumstances, because she or he has learned that the same behaviour brings different consequences in different circumstances.

Adults often reward children for behaving in accordance with their gender role. So a boy who continues playing football when he is hurt will be congratulated for being brave, and a girl who plays at feeding her dolls may be told what a good mother she will be.

Similarly with aggressive or antisocial behaviour, if a boy acts aggressively, having seen his father act in an aggressive or antisocial way, he may find that the other boys reinforce this behaviour by treating him with respect (or fear), and this might make him feel powerful. He will enjoy this reinforcement and this will increase the likelihood that he will behave in the same way again.

If criminals learn how to be criminals by observing and imitating the behaviour of others, this might explain the evidence showing that crime runs in families.

So, Bandura would claim that the child who has seen her parents being kind and caring, giving to charity, caring for the environment, being kind to animals, will tend to be the same. However, the child who has seen problems being faced with violence, arguments occurring, wrongdoing being punished by hitting, will tend to grow up to be more aggressive, and so on. They will learn violent ways of addressing the world.

Bandura's research on aggression

Albert Bandura conducted a series of laboratory experiments that studied the effect on children of watching an adult behave aggressively. For instance, Bandura and colleagues (1961) arranged for an adult to hit and kick a large inflatable doll (called a 'Bobo doll') while a child was in the room. Afterwards the child had the opportunity to play with a range of toys, including the doll, while the adult was present. Children in the control condition saw the adult models behaving without any aggression even when they got frustrated.

While each of the children was playing afterwards they were observed through a one-way mirror, and the number of incidents of aggression was noted. A summary of the main findings is given below.

- Higher levels of aggression were recorded in participants who had seen a model of the same sex.
- Boys performed more acts of aggression than girls.
- Boys showed much more verbal and physical aggression when they witnessed the male model rather than the female model.
- Girls showed much more verbal aggression when they witnessed the female model rather than the male model.
- Comments from the children indicated their awareness of what was appropriate behaviour, as some said 'Ladies shouldn't do things like that.'
- Children who had seen the model punished after being aggressive showed lower levels of aggression than those who saw the model rewarded.
- When participants were asked to reproduce as much of the model's behaviour as they could remember, the majority were able to do so accurately regardless of whether the model had been reinforced or punished. Some children had not previously been aggressive towards the doll when they had the chance, even though they could do so accurately when asked. These children had learned the behaviour even though they did not imitate it.

Figure 1.7 This sequence of photographs shows the aggressive behaviour of a boy and girl after they had watched the behaviour of an aggressive female model

Source: Bandura *et al*. (1961)

In later experiments, Bandura changed this procedure. In the **experimental condition** he showed children a *film* of someone being aggressive to the doll. Children in the **control condition** watched a non-violent film. The results indicated how powerful the media can be when shaping our behaviour. This raises the question of what role the media might be playing in encouraging aggression and violence in society. The presentation of aggression and violence in films, cartoons, TV programmes, computer games and books provides models that children and adults may imitate.

CORE STUDY: Mednick *et al.* (1984)

Mednick, S.A., Gabrielli, W.F. and Hutchings B. (1984) Genetic influences in criminal convictions: evidence from an adoption cohort. Science, *224, pp. 891–894.*

Candidates should be able to:

- describe Mednick *et al.*'s adoption study into the genetic basis of criminal behaviour

- outline the limitations of Mednick *et al.*'s study.

The aim of this study was to investigate whether people become criminals because of their genes or because of the environment in which they are brought up. If genetics could explain criminal behaviour, the children whose biological parents had been involved in criminal behaviour were more likely to be criminals themselves, even if their adoptive parents were law-abiding. On the other hand, if criminality was a result of environment, the children who had been adopted by law-abiding families were less likely to become involved in criminal activity.

Population
The authors found that 14,427 adoptees were included on a register of non-familiar adoptions (adopted by people other than their family members) which had taken place in a small northern European nation between 1927 and 1947. They then looked at court convictions as an indicator of criminal involvement.

Sample
The authors looked at the adoptees who had court convictions (total number 65,516) and further excluded them from the sample if:

- there was no record of place of birth

- there was no record of date of birth

- the biological father could not be traced

- the child was adopted by a single woman

- the child was born before 1895.

This left a remaining 13,185, of whom 6,129 were male and 7,065 were female.

Method

Information on the remaining adoptees' adoptive and biological parents was collected. The data was compiled and put in a table (see Table 1.5).

Family member	Number identified	Conviction rate by number of convictions			
		0	1	2	>2
Male adoptees	6,129	0.841	0.088	0.029	0.049
Female adoptees	7,065	0.972	0.020	0.005	0.003
Adoptive fathers	13,918	0.938	0.046	0.008	0.008
Adoptive mothers	14,267	0.981	0.015	0.002	0.002
Biological fathers	10,604	0.714	0.129	0.056	0.102
Biological mothers	12,300	0.911	0.064	0.012	0.013

Table 1.5 Conviction rates of completely identified members of the adoptees' families
Source: Mednick *et al.* (1984) Science *224: 891*

Results

1. The conviction rates for the biological fathers of the male adoptees (MAs) and female adoptees (FAs) are higher than for their adoptive fathers.

2. Most of the adoptive fathers who were convicted of criminal activity were only convicted once and had a lower level of criminality than the population as a whole, while the adoptees and their biological fathers were more recidivistic (likely to relapse into reoffending).

The authors then examined the relationship between the convictions of the parents and the MAs. They excluded the FAs as their conviction rates were much lower in number.

They then separated their population into subgroups and looked at the links between the biological parents, adoptive parents, whether they were convicted or not, and the percentage of their sons who were also convicted of a criminal offence.

3. The conclusion was that, the closer the biological relationship, the higher the level of MA convictions. The authors found a statistically significant link between convicted biological fathers and their adopted children.

Table 1.6 shows which groups were compared and indicates that:

- 13.5 per cent of the sons of non-convicted biological parents who were adopted by non-convicted adoptive parents received a criminal conviction

- 14.7 per cent of the sons of convicted adoptive parents and non-convicted biological parents received a criminal conviction

- 20 per cent of the sons of convicted biological parents and non-convicted adoptive parents received a criminal conviction

- 24.5 per cent of the sons of convicted biological parents and convicted adoptive parents received a criminal conviction.

Convicted biological parents	Convicted adoptive parents	Non-convicted biological parents	Non-convicted adoptive parents	Percentage of sons convicted
		✗	✗	13.5%
	✗	✗		14.7%
✗			✗	20%
✗	✗			24.5%

Table 1.6 The relationship between the convicted MAs and their families

4. If the biological parents were reoffenders, the MAs were shown to be more likely to reoffend (property crimes such as theft, but not violent crimes). This gives more support to the genetic basis for criminality.

If brothers who had been adopted into different families were both involved in criminal activity, this supports the idea that there is a genetic component to crime.

Relationship between siblings	Concordance rates (how likely they were to both be convicted)
Unrelated (different mothers and fathers)	8.5%
Half brothers (one different parent)	12.9%
Full brothers (same mother and father)	20%

Table 1.7 Concordance rates between siblings and convictions

5. Table 1.7 shows that, the more genetically related the brothers were, the more likely they were to both become involved in crime.

Females have lower rates of conviction. The authors suggest that this may be because FAs have a greater biological predisposition for crime. They decided to look at criminal behaviour in the biological mother to see if this was more closely related to both the MAs and FAs than the criminal behaviour in the biological father.

6. The relationship between biological mother and their adopted sons or daughters being convicted is stronger than the relationship between the biological father and adoptee convictions.

7. This relationship is even stronger for mothers and daughters (the daughters of convicted biological mothers are more likely than sons to turn to crime).

8. Some adoptees who were raised in more affluent families were only slightly less likely to turn to crime. The biological relationship was a bigger influence on later criminal behaviour.

The authors' observations
The authors made the following observations.

- Although some adoptees were excluded from the data analysis because their families could not be traced, the authors suggest that their inclusion would not have altered the results.

- The authors acknowledge that the adoptees were taken from their parents at different times and had different experiences. They claim that these differences did not influence the likelihood that they would become criminals:

  - 25.3 per cent of the adoptees were placed in an adoptive home straight away

  - 74.7 per cent were placed in orphanages

  - 50.6 per cent of the children placed in orphanages were adopted in the first year and 12.8 per cent in the second year

  - 11.3 per cent were adopted after the age of two.

- Prospective adoptive parents were told about the convictions of the biological parents and it was thought that this may have affected the way they treated the adoptees, perhaps thinking they too might have become criminals. However, when the authors looked at the times when the adoptive parents were actually told (before or after the adoption) it made no difference to the rate of criminality of the adoptees.

Conclusions
The authors found a relationship between the criminal convictions of the biological parent and their adopted children. No relationship was found between the type of

crime of the biological parents and the adopted child. They concluded that some 'factor' was transmitted by criminal parents that increased the likelihood of their children becoming criminals.

Weaknesses
The study raises the following questions.

- The study was retrospective so none of the participants could be interviewed to clarify the data.

- Can we generalise from this sample to the population as a whole? Are they really representative?

- The conviction rates shown in this study may not have been accurate, as some people do not actually get caught.

- Do we know that the other adoptees' data (data not included in the study) were the same as those of the included adoptees, as the authors do not provide the statistics?

- Perhaps some of the adoptive parents had been criminals but had not been caught.

- The authors suggest that the girls were less likely to be affected by their environments and say that they must somehow have had a biological predisposition for crime. Why?

- Perhaps the women in the sample had got away with crimes (i.e. weren't convicted) because they were not perceived by the judges to be capable of criminal activities.

- How can we be sure that the early experiences of the criminal adoptees did not affect them? After all, a child going into a children's home is going to have very different early experiences to one being adopted straight away.

- It's difficult to see how a factor for 'being a criminal' can exist because there are so many behaviours that can be judged to be criminal, and some of these are perfectly acceptable in other cultures. Think about someone who steals money from others – if you are a market trader and you swindle someone out of a few pounds you might well end up in court, but if you are head of a major UK bank and you pay yourself hundreds of thousands of pounds while at the same time driving the bank into near bankruptcy, then you will not end up in court but with a large payout to leave your job. Crime is a difficult concept to nail down – the bigger the act, the less you are likely to be caught or even called a criminal.

APPLICATION OF RESEARCH INTO CRIMINAL BEHAVIOUR: crime reduction

Candidates should be able to:
- explain how psychological research relates to crime reduction, e.g. biological perspective on the use of prisons, implications of research for crime prevention, reinforcement and rehabilitation.

CRIME REDUCTION

The biological perspective on the use of prisons

If people are 'born criminals' this has significant repercussions for the use of prisons as a way of reducing crime. If we take, for example, Lombroso's suggestion that people are criminals because of their physical characteristics, then the only way of managing these criminals is to remove them from society by locking them away, as any method of rehabilitation will be pointless.

Some criminals are deemed to be 'insane', because they are incapable of thinking or behaving in a rational or acceptable way. As we have seen, this can be linked to imbalances in brain chemicals, which, in turn, might result in a mental illness such as psychopathy or schizophrenia. Should these criminals be imprisoned with others who have no 'excuse' for their behaviour? Surely, we have a moral obligation to treat these individuals using medical techniques rather than simply locking them away? Perhaps hospitalisation is a more appropriate environment for them rather than prison.

Broadmoor, Rampton and Ashworth are high-security psychiatric hospitals in England; Carstairs is a similar institution in Scotland. They house the most dangerous patients, most of whom have been convicted of serious crimes or are considered unfit to plead. During their stay, prisoners may receive medication together with additional therapies such as counselling. In the past, institutions like these 'treated' prisoners using surgical interventions. Lobotomies were regularly performed on inmates to remove the parts of the brain that were believed to cause criminal acts (see Figure 1.8).

If all criminality could be put down to biological causes, then perhaps prisons would at best provide a kind of storage facility for people with the wrong sort of physiology. However, psychology has indicated that the reasons for criminal behaviour are often very complex and therefore using prisons in this way may contain the inmates but will have little impact on the thoughts and subsequent behaviour of the majority of offenders.

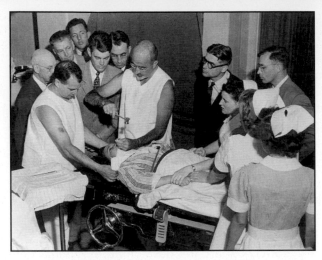

Figure 1.8 Prisoner at Vacaville Penitentiary in California being prepared for a lobotomy in 1961. At the time, many psychiatrists believed that 'criminal' behaviour was lodged in certain parts of the brain, and lobotomies were frequently carried out on prisoners

Among the many reasons for challenging the biological explanation of crime is the relative failure of any of the biological treatments (such as the lobotomy) to reduce crime rates. The approach also goes against our experience of life, which tells us that we have some control over our lives and can choose to do bad things or good things.

Implications of psychological research on crime reduction

Research has indicated that most criminality is not due purely to biology but is more likely to be due to a mixture of both nature (biology) and nurture (social and life experiences). Although psychology cannot influence biology directly, it can influence our understanding and subsequent treatment of criminal behaviours.

Consider the following suggestions.

● Children are more likely to identify with the same-sex parent in order to reduce the anxiety caused by the Oedipus and Electra complex. WIth any sort of disruption to this process, high levels of anxiety might lead to unusual or extreme behaviours. We also know from social learning theory that children learn by observation, especially when the role model is of the same sex and more powerful. This has implications for parents who might need guidance on how to be the most effective role model for their children. It also suggests that teachers and other significant adults have a responsibility to act as positive role models.

- Rewards for certain behaviours are likely to increase the likelihood of them being repeated, therefore we should ensure that the rewards for remaining on the right side of the law outweigh the rewards for engaging in criminal behaviour.

Today the management of *convicted* criminals involves access to psychologists who work with their thoughts, feelings and patterns of behaviour, and who help prisoners cope with any anxiety or trauma that has been the result of early experiences. They also learn life and work-related skills, the aim being to allow them to be rehabilitated and return to society without the need to continue criminal activity. Unfortunately, current rates of reoffending suggest that prisons have not yet become a really effective way of managing criminal behaviour and need to develop further.

You will probably have realised that the reasons why people turn to crime are complicated not only by their biology but also by their life experiences, their social relationships, the type of people who act as role models, and so on. It is also worth noting that people who commit crimes probably don't see themselves as criminal. Some of them will see themselves as being in a regular job where one of the important things is not to let the police know what you are doing. And, in many ways, their behaviour and attitudes will be very similar to those of some people at the top of major companies such as UK banks just before the great financial crash of 2008.

In Chapter 2, on cognitive psychology, you will begin to realise how our experiences influence the way we see things, and how the way our memory works affects the things we remember.

Cognitive psychology

Cognitive psychology aims to understand the internal mental processes involved in interpreting and making sense of the world around us, including why we forget and how we can improve remembering. It also considers the way we interpret what we see and how our past experiences can actually affect the way we understand what we see.

- The first section of this chapter looks at the way our memories work, and considers how we take in and store information. The study relating to this section focuses on how we are often likely to remember either the first or last pieces of information we are told, but forget much of the information that comes in the middle.
- The second section of this chapter looks at perception: the process of interpreting, organising and making sense of sensory information. The study of visual perception considers how we make sense of the information that comes into our brain through our eyes. Psychologists have investigated the extent to which visual perception develops as a result of our experiences, or whether most of our visual abilities are innate, and this is a major theme of this section. The study relating to this part of the chapter considers how information stored in our memory can influence our judgement of size.

MEMORY

OVERVIEW

Without memory we would be unable to do many of the things we take for granted, to use words, to dress ourselves, to recognise a familiar voice, even to recognise our own face in the mirror. Without memory, everything we experience would seem to be experienced for the first time; it would be completely new to us. As well as giving a background to some of the work on memory, this chapter considers reasons why we forget and some ideas for helping us remember, which is particularly useful for students who are about to sit exams!

KEY CONCEPTS

The OCR examination requires candidates to be able to:

- describe information processing – input, encoding, storage, retrieval, output
- distinguish between accessibility and availability problems in memory.

THE STAGES OF MEMORY

When you are watching a film your brain has to process the information you receive. The images you see enter your eyes as light waves, what you hear enters your ears as sound waves. In order that you can make use of it, this information goes through the following three stages: encoding, storage and retrieval.

Encoding

Information enters through our senses (through our eyes or ears) and is changed (or encoded) so that we can make sense of it. Light waves are converted into images (see the section on perceptual abilities, page 63), sound waves are converted into music and words, words are converted into meanings, and so on. Once encoded, the information can then be **stored**.

Storage

The **encoded** information is stored as a memory so it is available for use at some time in the future. Our memory for a word will include memory of what it sounds like, what it looks like and what it means. We store different types of information in different ways, and the way we store information affects how we **retrieve** it.

Retrieval

This occurs when we try to recover information from storage. If we 'can't remember' something it may be because we are unable to retrieve it. Have you ever gone to pick up something from another room, but when you get there cannot remember what it was? Returning to where you started from often enables you to retrieve the information. Sometimes we really think we have forgotten something – perhaps how to do something on a computer – then someone shows us what to do, and after only one demonstration we can remember the whole sequence. This is called **re-learning** – we seem to have almost remembered what to do but need a little extra help to remember it completely.

Output

Once we have retrieved the information from memory, this 'output' may result in us choosing to make some sort of response or take some sort of action.

CORE THEORY: multi-store model of memory

Candidates should be able to:

- distinguish between sensory store, short-term memory and long-term memory, with reference to duration and capacity

- describe the processes of attention and rehearsal

- explain how forgetting occurs through decay and displacement

- explain the criticisms of the multi-store model of memory

- consider the 'levels of processing' theory as an alternative theory, with specific reference to the importance of deep processing in memory.

ATKINSON AND SHIFFRIN'S MULTI-STORE MODEL OF MEMORY

One of the first psychologists, William James (1890), noticed that we either store information for a very short time or seem to retain it indefinitely. He made the distinction between what we now call **short-term memory** and **long-term memory**. This distinction forms the basis for Atkinson and Shiffrin's multi-store model of memory, which has been widely used as a framework for research.

The key features of Atkinson and Shiffrin's (1968) model

R.C. Atkinson and R.M. Shiffrin's model suggested that information passed into sensory store, then into short-term memory and, finally, into long-term memory.

Sensory store

Information enters the sensory store through our sense receptors (eyes, ears, nose, mouth and skin). This information is held as a 'fleeting' memory within these receptors, not at a central location; it lasts for a very short period of time and is then gone.

From this information, we select what we want to retain or process while all other information is lost, although it is not clear how this happens. This process is necessary as we are bombarded with so much information that we would go into a state of overload if we tried to process all that information at the same time. Look around the room that you are in. There are probably many different things to see and hear. If you have to 'process' the information about each one – for example, deciding what it is, what it does, where it came from – then you would spend far too long doing this and not achieve anything else.

This memory seems to work outside our conscious awareness, but we can sometimes bring it into conscious awareness. For example, when someone says something to you and you haven't really paid attention, you ask them to repeat what they said and, just before they say it again, you remember what it was.

What we do is to somehow select the information that is of interest, relevant or unusual. In fact, **attention** is a cognitive process whereby we select a piece of information while ignoring other things. The information that enters sensory memory must somehow be processed in order to allow this process of selection to take place. It is such an amazing process and is so instantaneous that we are not aware of it happening.

Short-term memory (STM)

Atkinson and Shiffrin proposed that the sensory information we have attended to (and then selected as being important) is passed into short-term memory (STM). The remaining unimportant information simply **decays** and is lost.

Only a small amount of information can be held in short-term memory – up to about seven plus or minus two items – so new information coming in pushes out (or **displaces**) information already held. It is generally stored for long enough to enable us to use it – for example, retaining a phone number long enough to dial it, although it may be forgotten soon after. It is also the memory store that allows us to have a conversation with another person. You can't remember the whole content of a conversation but will be able to remember enough to respond.

Information can be held in STM only for up to 30 seconds, but if it is **rehearsed** – which means repeated over and over again – then it transfers to long-term memory. Here it may remain indefinitely and can be retrieved for future use.

Long-term memory (LTM)

Some of the things we experience or learn as we grow up stay with us for very long periods, and some for the whole of our lives. This information will have been transferred to long-term memory (LTM). Information taken into long-term memory is information that is meaningful to us (**semantic information**), or someone's spoken words or music (**acoustic information**), or visual images (**iconic information**). Part of the information may be lost, distorted or overlaid with later material, so it is not as if memory is like a tape recorder. You have probably realised, when trying to remember something that happens on a regular basis, that you mix up memories of one event with the next.

Psychologists believe that the capacity of long-term memory is infinite as no one has ever been in a position where they cannot take in any more information, although sometimes it might feel – say, if you are revising – that you cannot learn anything else.

ACTIVITY continued

7										
6	8									
9	3	5								
4	2	1	3							
5	8	7	3	1						
6	2	8	5	9	7					
9	4	3	8	2	6	5				
2	8	6	4	9	5	3	7			
8	6	9	4	6	3	2	4	8		
9	5	7	5	6	3	2	9	4	3	
2	4	7	6	9	5	8	3	6	3	2

When your participant has reached the limit of their memory, try asking them what the first digit was that they were given. They are unlikely to remember the first digit because it will have been displaced by later information.

Decay

As time passes, information we have stored is often forgotten. The memory trace involves tiny changes in the brain, and if the memory is to be retained this trace must be strengthened, which is what happens in rehearsal. Unless it is strengthened, the trace decays – that is, it breaks down and fades. This is an explanation for information loss in short-term memory but it has also been used to explain some long-term memory loss, in so far as lack of use of information in long-term memory may also lead to decay of the memory trace.

One of the strengths of trace decay theory is that it explains re-learning; this is when you learn something, think you have forgotten it but, when you look at it again, it comes back to you really quickly. It is as if going through something just once or twice strengthens a memory that had started to decay.

Criticisms of the multi-store model

Although the model described in Table 2.1 does provide a simple description of memory processes, and research supports the characteristics of short-term memory and long-term memory described above, it has been widely criticised for its focus on memory for new facts, such as word lists, numbers or nonsense syllables. This is why the model seems to explain how we remember a telephone number until we can dial it, but it cannot explain many of our everyday experiences of memory. Rehearsal is one way by which we transfer information from short- to long-term memory, but it is not the only way.

For instance, why are we able to recall information that we did not rehearse, yet are unable to recall information that we have rehearsed? Why can we remember how to swim, which is not learned as 'pieces' of information? Why could you read this page several times and yet recall very little of it? Because Atkinson and Shiffrin's model cannot provide satisfactory answers to these questions, researchers have explored a number of other possible explanations. We will look briefly at another theory that has been developed as an alternative explanation as to why we store only some information in long-term memory.

THE LEVELS OF PROCESSING THEORY

If rehearsal is not the only process we use to transfer information from short- to long-term memory, perhaps the reason why information is transferred is due to the amount of processing we give to pieces of information. F.I.M. Craik and R.S. Lockhart (1972) supported this view with their 'model' of memory, which is known as the levels of processing theory. They argued that it is not rehearsal as such that is important, it is more to do with what we do with the material during that rehearsal (i.e. how well it is processed) and it is this alone that will determine the duration of the memory. The methods we use for this processing are those we have already talked about when we looked at encoding – that is, what information looks like, what it sounds like and what it means.

Craik and Lockhart claim that iconic processing (what something looks like) is the most shallow form of processing. Acoustic processing (what something sounds like) is the next level and requires more processing, and if you then take into account what this thing actually means (semantic processing), you will have to process the information much more deeply.

The following activity gives an example of a way you can test this out.

ACTIVITY

Compose a list of about 21 words – for example, house, egg, shoes. Divide the list into three so that you have seven words in each list. For the first seven words, you should have a question that asks about the structure of the word (e.g. 'Is the word in capital letters or lower case?'). For the second seven words,

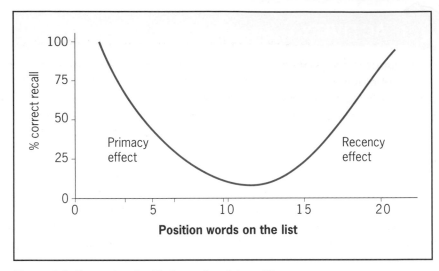

Figure 2.2 Example of a U-shaped serial position curve

The curve shown in Figure 2.2 is known as the 'U-shaped serial position curve'. This curve illustrates the primacy and recency effects when people are asked to learn a list of 20 words and freely recall them (recall them in any order). The words at the beginning of the list and the words at the end of the list are more likely to be recalled than those in the middle. The explanation for these effects is as follows.

The primacy effect can be explained by participants having longer to rehearse the information before the end of the learning period, and to transfer the information into LTM, whereas the last words in the list are more likely to be retained in STM. The information in the middle of the list would not have had enough rehearsal to transfer it to LTM, but would have been displaced by more information coming into STM due to the limited capacity of STM.

CORE STUDY: Terry (2005)

Terry, W.S. (2005) Serial position effects in recall of television commercials. Journal of General Psychology, *132, pp. 151–163.*

Candidates should be able to:

- describe Terry's experiment on the serial position effect in recall of TV commercials
- outline the limitations of Terry's study.

If we are likely to remember the first and last pieces of information given, this will have implications for commercial breaks on television. Perhaps viewers are more likely to remember the first advertisements shown and the last ones before the programme starts again, and forget the ones in the middle. Terry therefore questions whether the classic U-shaped serial position curve will occur with the recall of television commercials, so that viewers remember the first and last ones seen, but forget the ones in the middle of the commercial break.

Two naturalistic studies (M. R. Banaji and R. G. Crowder 1989; X. Zhao 1997) have been conducted by contacting viewers and asking them to recall advertisements they had seen in their own homes. Both studies found that the primacy effect was more evident, although, as the studies were not controlled in the same way as laboratory experiments, it was suggested that the viewers may have, in some cases, watched the first commercials and then left the room.

Another confounding variable (see Chapter 6, page 250) would be the distinctiveness of the advert. Perhaps it was visually dramatic or relevant to the area where it was broadcast, and therefore would attract more attention than the other adverts. The participants in naturalistic studies may remember the advert as being at the beginning of a commercial break, whereas it may have been in the middle but would have been remembered as being first or last.

The aim of this research was to try to control the confounding variables present in Zhao's and Banaji and Crowder's studies by conducting an experiment in a laboratory and seeing if their results were **replicated**.

Experiment 1
Design
A laboratory experiment with independent groups.

Participants
A total of 39 undergraduate college students (22 women and 17 men) were tested in groups of six to eight in a small classroom.

Materials
Four lists of 15 television commercials were put together, giving a total of 60 adverts.

- The adverts were made 10 months before the experiment was conducted *(to ensure the adverts were not too familiar).**

- The lists were put together as follows:
  - Two lists of 15 × 15 second commercials = 3.75 minutes long (short list)
  - Two lists of 15 × 30 second commercials = 7.5 minutes long (long list).

Text in italics was not reported in the actual study.

- The author also moved the first six to eight commercials, in a block, to the end of the list for one of the 3.75 minute lists and one of the 7.5 minute lists *(to ensure there were no order effects: see Chapter 6, pages 252–3)*

- The adverts were different in the short and long lists *(so that participants did not memorise an advert seen in a previous list)*.

- The categories of product were not repeated within a list *(to prevent confusion between products)*.

Procedure

The students were informed about the experiment and read the informed consent letter. They were told that the study was to test their memory for brand names immediately after they had been shown the adverts.

They were also told that some lists would be tested immediately after they had been seen while others would not *(suggesting that they might not be tested on all lists)*.

Half the students, in groups of six to eight, watched one short list and one long list. They were then asked to remember as many of the adverts as they could (free recall). After that, they were then shown the second two lists.

Once they had seen them, they worked on a page of verbal SATs (Scholastic Assessment Tests) practice items for three minutes. They were then asked to complete their research participant forms for a further three minutes.

Then, unexpectedly, they were asked to recall the last two lists. For an item to be scored correct, the brand name of the item had to be recalled.

They were then debriefed and given information about the experimental hypothesis.

Results

The author divided the adverts into three blocks (first five seen, second five seen, final five seen) for ease of analysis.

1. *Calculation A – immediate recall:* he calculated the results for immediate recall.

2. *Calculation B – final testing:* he calculated the results for delayed recall *(recall after participants had done the SATs practice items and participant forms)*.

3. *Calculation C – final after immediate:* he compared the results for immediate recall with the delayed recall *(to see if time affected what had been remembered)*.

The results were as follows:

- Length of advert had no effect on participants' ability to remember it.

- Primacy and recency effects were obvious with immediate recall, with more items being remembered from the beginning and end of the sequence of adverts.

- More adverts were remembered from the final block (recency effects) with immediate recall.

- More adverts were remembered from the first block (primacy effects) with delayed recall.

Conclusions

The results of this study confirmed the results of naturalistic studies showing primacy effects but not recency effects in delayed recall.

By testing the immediate recall of the participants, the author showed that the last items were noticed and remembered at first even if they were forgotten when tested later in the experiment. Because the author had varied the order of the advertisements and found no difference between them, he had demonstrated that the results were to do with the way people's memories worked rather than the characteristics of the advertisements themselves.

Experiment 2

Participants

A different group of 27 students (approximately 57 per cent were women but not all identified their gender), tested in groups of eight to ten.

Materials

A 21-minute pre-recorded comedy programme.

Three blocks of 30-second commercials recorded 18 months before the study. (Two of the blocks of adverts had been used in Experiment 1.)

Procedure

A comedy programme was recorded. Three 30-second commercials were inserted after 4 minutes, 8 minutes and 15 minutes (natural breaks in the comedy). The programme was then stopped at 18 minutes.

The adverts were again varied in order of presentation *(to prevent order effects)*.

The participants were told that there would be a memory test at the end of the session. They then viewed the recorded programme and adverts. At the end, they were asked to recall the ones they had seen.

Results

The results again showed that the adverts seen at the beginning in all of the lists were more likely to be recalled than the others.

Experiment 3

In this experiment, the author tested recognition of brand names rather than recall, as he suggested that recognition is a better test of memory because participants might have remembered the advertisement but not been able to remember the product name.

Materials
Three lists of commercials embedded in a television programme.

A recognition test that mixed the 45 brand names from the adverts with 30 distractors, which were also brand names taken from adverts.

Participants
Another group of 23 students (56 per cent were women but not all identified their gender).

Procedure
Participants watched the television programme. They were then shown the recognition list, and were told that some of the adverts they had seen were on the list and some were not (not how many of each there were), and were asked to identify adverts they had seen.

Results

- Correctly identified items *and* incorrectly identified distractors were totalled.

- In some cases, participants achieved full scores (ceiling effects).

- The results showed the same decline in recall for the last items presented.

- Lower numbers of commercials were recalled as more lists were presented.

Discussion

- The author acknowledges that the adverts may well have been familiar to the participants prior to the study. He also acknowledges that the sound, visual quality and distinctiveness of adverts varied.

- He reminds us that the primacy effect occurred no matter what advertisement came first.

- He suggests that **proactive interference** may explain the problems with remembering words later in the lists. (Proactive interference occurs when something you already know interferes with your ability to take in new information.)

- He also mentions that the results of this study have implications for television advertising, suggesting that advertisers will be interested in the position their advertisement will take in a commercial break.

- He concludes by saying that the results of this study support the results of previous laboratory and field experiments.

Limitations

The author acknowledged some limitations of the study. For example, he admitted that laboratory experiments are not ecologically valid (although the author tried to make parts of the study as lifelike as possible – for example, showing the adverts embedded in a television programme). Also, the participants were all students and therefore not representative of the entire population.

- The students were in a classroom, knowing they were taking part in some research. Perhaps they did not take the research seriously.

- There were not equal numbers of males and females.

- Some participants were not able to give fully informed consent.

APPLICATION OF RESEARCH INTO MEMORY: memory aids

Candidates should be able to:
- explain how psychological research relates to memory aids, e.g. use of cues and retrieval failure, use of imagery and meaning, mind mapping and organisation.

IMPROVING MEMORY

When we are trying to remember stored information, it has to be brought back into conscious awareness. Often, information can be easily recalled but, at times, it seems that that information is locked away. When psychologists talk about remembering, they often use a technique called **free recall**, whereby people do not have to remember information in any particular order and do not have any cues to help. They also use **recognition**, which involves trying to identify something we have seen before from a large array. Answering a multiple-choice question involves recognition, whereas writing an essay from a title involves using free recall where it is necessary to delve into the recesses of memory for facts to write about.

From the vast amount of research on memory, psychologists have been able to suggest techniques to help people improve their memory. These techniques, known as mnemonics (or memory aids), usually require working with the material to be remembered or linking it with material already in long-term memory. This aids in the encoding of new material and in its retrieval, so it is obviously helpful for students who want to remember the material they are studying.

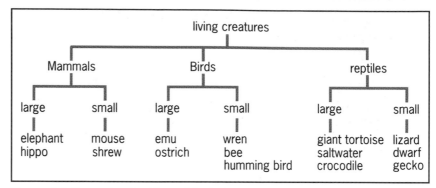

Figure 2.4 Example of a hierarchical structure

from four categories (animals, professions, names and vegetables) but were presented in a random order. Results showed that participants recalled words in clusters from the same category, suggesting that we spontaneously organise information by meaning.

Mind mapping

The idea of mind maps came from Tony Buzan and originated in the late 1960s. They are a sort of diagram that is used to represent information, originating from a central key word or idea. The ideas branch from the centre and are linked together in a sort of tree structure, with the central concepts leading to more and more minor concepts. They involve pictures and colour, and are therefore a helpful tool to support learning, especially for people who find it easy to remember visual rather than spoken information.

Tony Buzan suggests the following seven steps to making a mind map.

1. Start in the centre of a blank page turned sideways. This allows the map to develop in all directions.
2. The central idea is usually represented with an image or picture in order to trigger imagination. Also, pictures are often more able to convey meaning than words.
3. Colours are very useful, and make the map more interesting to create and look at.
4. The main branches are connected to the central image, and the second- and third-level branches are connected to the first and second levels, and so on. This gives the mind map associations to work from, links things together and gives a kind of hierarchical structure.
5. The branches should be curved rather than straight, because curved lines are more interesting to the brain.
6. There should be only one key word per line.
7. Images should be used throughout the map because images convey more meaning than words.

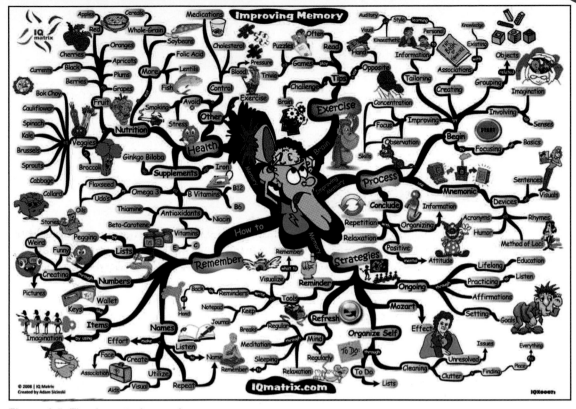

Figure 2.5 Five keys to improving your memory

PERCEPTION

OVERVIEW

When we look at something, light rays enter the pupils of each eye, projecting an image on to the retina at the back of the eye (see Figure 2.6, below). Not only are the images small, blurred and upside down, but there are two of them. From this crude sensory input, we are able to perceive one clear, three-dimensional coloured image, which is the right way up. The process whereby these crude images are interpreted and understood is called perception. Perception is the process of interpreting, organising and elaborating sensations, and it is the subject of this part of the chapter.

KEY CONCEPTS

Sensation, perception, depth cues
The OCR examination requires candidates to be able to:

- describe the difference between sensation and perception using shape constancy, colour constancy and visual illusions
- explain depth cues, including linear perspective, height in plane, relative size, superimposition and texture gradient.

PERCEPTION

Perception does not simply refer to our understanding of sensations entering the body through the eyes. In fact, when we take in any sort of sensory information, whether it is through our eyes, ears, fingertips, nose or mouth, it is necessary for us to process and identify what it is. A series of individual instruments playing at the same time can be perceived as a concerto, while various chemical compounds released from foodstuffs can be perceived as a roast dinner, and so on.

The study of visual perception considers how we make sense of the information that comes into our brain through our eyes. Psychologists have investigated the extent to which visual perception develops as a result of our experiences, or whether most of our visual abilities are innate. This is a major theme of this chapter.

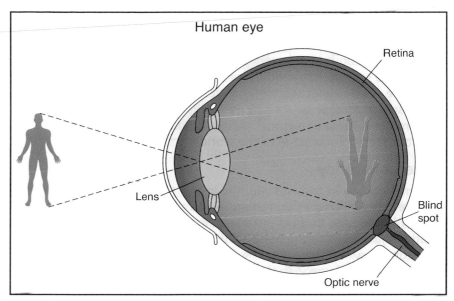

Human eye

Retina

Lens

Blind spot

Optic nerve

Figure 2.6 Images are inverted on their way to the retina at the back of the eye

PERCEPTUAL ABILITIES

The sensory information for vision is the light waves that, when they strike the retina, are changed into electrical impulses that are transmitted to the brain. We make sense of this information, interpreting it, organising it and elaborating on it. The brain is also able to fill in any gaps in our sensation in order to make an object appear whole.

ACTIVITY

Look at a wall in front of you and, while looking at it, wave your hand from side to side in front of your face. You are still able to see the wall even though the image on your retina changes from wall to hand to wall to hand. The brain fills in the missing information that has been disrupted by the moving hand. Similarly, are you aware that the image you are focusing on is actually being disrupted on a regular basis by your blinking?

Subliminal advertising

An American market researcher called Jim Vicary convinced the owner of a cinema to flash phrases for 0.03 of a second such as 'Hungry? Eat Popcorn' and 'Drink Coca-Cola' during a film. As a result, sales of popcorn and Coca-Cola rose considerably. The cinema-goers did not have any awareness of the messages they had been given, although they seemed to have actually perceived the messages and processed the information. This suggests that there are different levels of perception (both conscious and unconscious). This links with the work of Gibson (1950, 1966, 1979) when he suggested that we unconsciously process information from the environment in order to help us to get around (see page 74).

Subliminal messages were also used in horror films to scare people further. The 1974 film, *The Exorcist*, contained a subliminal picture of a death mask, while other films had pictures of skulls and blood presented for less than a second. *The Exorcist* was considered by many to be one of the best horror films ever made (although others found it very, very disturbing, including the author!). Whether this was due to the subliminal messages, we cannot be sure.

Research into subliminal messages is mixed, although much of the research suggests they have a degree of effectiveness. However, due to ethical concerns, subliminal advertising was banned in the 1950s. Choosing whether to watch an advertisement or not is our free choice but, because we don't know about subliminal messages, we are deceived into watching them, thus removing our right to decide.

Developmental psychology

Developmental psychology is concerned with the ways in which people change over their lifespan, from birth to maturity. Developmental psychologists consider how much of a child's development is influenced by nature and how much is affected by the child's experiences (nurture).

- The first section in this chapter looks at the attachment that develops between a parent and a child, and considers Bowlby's theory that mothers and babies have an innate biological need for each other. The section also considers whether behaviourist theory provides an alternative explanation to this maternal relationship. It also considers what happens when attachments go wrong. The core study for this section looks at the relationship between the nature of the attachment formed by a parent and a child, and whether this influences the types of relationship we have as adults.
- The second section looks at cognitive development, particularly Piaget's theory about how children's thinking develops. It also considers Vygotsky's theory as an alternative. The core study for this section is Piaget's experiment into the conservation of number.

ATTACHMENT

OVERVIEW

An attachment can be defined as 'a close emotional relationship with another person'.

The newborn infant is utterly dependent on others if it is to survive. It needs others to provide food, warmth and protection. In order for the infant to get what it needs, it uses innate behaviours such as crying, making eye contact, reaching and grasping, which in turn invite carers to respond to its needs. Attachments between the baby and the potential carer form from this interaction.

For the first three months of life, most babies respond equally to any caregiver, but then they start to respond more to the people who are familiar to them. So a baby may wave its arms or smile when it sees its father's face, but there will be little reaction from the baby when it sees a stranger. The baby continues to respond most to those it interacts with frequently until about six or seven months of age. It then begins to show a special preference – an attachment – to certain people. We consider that the baby has formed an attachment to someone when it shows two particular behaviours:

1. **separation protest** – if the baby cries when its mother leaves the room, we conclude that the baby feels insecure when the mother is out of sight
2. **stranger anxiety** – if a stranger comes close to the baby and it moves away from the stranger and towards another person, we conclude that it is fearful of strangers and gains security from this person.

Some babies show these behaviours much more frequently and intensely than others, but nevertheless they are seen as evidence that the baby has formed an attachment when it looks to that person for security, comfort and protection. Such an attachment has usually developed by the age of one.

THE SECURITY OF ATTACHMENTS

The nature of a child's attachment to its caregiver will depend on how confident it is that the 'special person' will provide what it needs. The security of a one-year-old's attachment to its mother was tested by Mary Ainsworth in a number of studies using what she called the 'Strange Situation' studies. These were controlled observations in which observers noted children's behaviour when mothers and strangers came in to and left the room. Ainsworth concluded that the type of attachment children showed could be classed as secure or insecure – but there were two types of insecurity.

Figure 3.1 This baby may be showing stranger fear

One of the first studies Ainsworth conducted was undertaken in Baltimore, USA, in 1971. Details of the percentage of children showing the three attachment types from this study are shown in Table 3.1. Later studies indicated similar percentages – for example, J. Campos, K. Barrett, M. Lamb, H. Goldsmith and C. Sternberg (1983) summarised a number of American studies, which classified children into the three attachment types. They concluded that, in America, 62 per cent of children were found to be secure, 23 per cent were anxious-avoidant and 15 per cent were anxious-ambivalent.

form an attachment, and that there was a critical period between about six months and three years of age during which the baby can most easily form an attachment. Because the critical period is biologically programmed, Bowlby argued that if an attachment has not formed during this time, it will probably be too late.

Bowlby's stress on the importance of this attachment is underlined by his prediction that if it failed to develop, or was damaged in the first five years of life, there would be long-term and irreversible problems in the child's emotional, social and cognitive development. He called this 'maternal deprivation', and we look at this in more detail later in the chapter (page 94).

Criticisms of Bowlby's theory of attachment

Bowlby's theory of attachment offered a comprehensive explanation for the development of attachments. His evidence was crucial in changing childcare practices in, for example, hospitals. For the first time, parents were encouraged to be with their child in hospital.

Bowlby's theory generated much research, some of which challenged or modified it. For example, children with a poor attachment to their mother do not always have poor relationships with others, whether adults or peers. Critics also argue that the reason for good relationships with the mother and others, or for poor relationships with the mother and others, could depend on how good children are at forming relationships with anyone.

Figure 3.2 Bowlby would say these orphans are likely to have suffered permanent damage because they have experienced maternal deprivation

Below we look at research that criticises Bowlby's claim for a critical period and for monotropy, the special nature of the mother–child relationship.

Is there a critical period?

If children who are not able to form an attachment with their mothers are able to form attachments later in life, after the age of three, this refutes Bowlby's claim for a critical period for the development of an attachment.

Evidence that main attachments can form later comes from a longitudinal study by B. Tizard, J. Rees and J. Hodges (1978). They followed the development of children who had been in institutionalised care (residential nurseries) from only a few months of age until they were three years old. Some were then adopted, some returned to their mothers, some remained in the nursery. There was also a control group: these children had spent all their lives with their own families.

When assessed at eight years old, the institutionalised children who had been adopted had developed good attachments. Their social and intellectual development was better than that of children who had left the nursery to return to their own families. This suggests that there is not a critical period for the development of attachments, and also that the best place for children is not always with their own mothers, which is what Bowlby claimed.

Is there a special mother–child relationship?

Several aspects of this claim have been criticised; the research by H.R. Schaffer and P.E. Emerson (1964) is an example. They used naturalistic observation and interviews over 12 months to discover more about how infants develop attachments during their first year or so of life. Their results contradict Bowlby because they found that:

- The mother was the main attachment figure for about half the children at 18 months old; for the rest, the father was the main figure.
- Many of the babies had more than one attachment by ten months old; attachment figures included the mother, father, grandparents, brothers, sisters and neighbours.
- Attachments were most likely to form with those who responded accurately to the baby's signals, which Schaffer and Emerson called 'sensitive responsiveness'. If the main carer ignored the baby's signals then there was often greater attachment to someone the baby saw less, but who responded to it more sensitively.

Michael Rutter (1982) evaluated Bowlby's ideas using a wide range of evidence, and concluded that the quality of the child's main attachments is actually very similar, although one attachment may be stronger than the rest. So children seem to form several attachments

CORE STUDY: Hazen and Shaver (1987)

Hazen, R.L. and Shaver, S. (1987) Romantic love conceptualised as an attachment process. Journal of Personality and Social Psychology *52, APA Journals, pp. 511–524.*

Candidates should be able to:

- describe Hazen and Shaver's survey of the relationship between attachment types and adult relationships

- outline the limitations of Hazen and Shaver's study.

Background

The introduction to the study describes aspects of Bowlby's work in a little more detail than we have previously outlined, in order to lead the reader to the aims of the study. Therefore we will consider additional aspects of Bowlby's work, as cited by the authors.

The authors begin by citing Bowlby's work and his interest in the way infants become emotionally attached to their primary caregivers and distressed when they are separated from them. Bowlby believed that 'attachment behaviour' influences a person's behaviour throughout their lives. The authors explain that they were interested in whether or not Bowlby's theory of attachment could help to explain romantic love. They suggest that romantic love is experienced differently by different people, according to their early infant experiences of attachment.

Bowlby's theory developed from observing infants and young children who were separated from their primary caregiver (usually the mother) for various lengths of time. He also considered the work of others when looking at the emotional responses of primates to the same situation. He noticed that, following separation, the infants went through a series of emotional reactions:

- protest – crying, searching for the caregiver and resistance to others trying to console it

- despair – the child becomes passive and sad

- detachment – which was an active disregard for mother and avoidance if she returns (not shown in primates).

Bowlby (1973) summarised his theory into three propositions as follows.

1. When a person is confident that their 'attachment figure' will be available when needed, the person will not be as fearful or anxious as others who do not have that confidence.

2. Confidence in the availability of an attachment figure is slowly built up during the

person's childhood into adolescence. This confidence is likely to remain relatively unchanged throughout the rest of the person's life.

3. A person's expectations as to how accessible and responsive their attachment figure will be generally reflect their early experiences.

The authors go on to explain that a secure attachment relationship is not always guaranteed, and a mother's sensitivity and responsiveness to her child's signals during the first year of life are important for future relationships. Table 3.3 provides a more detailed description of Ainsworth's categories of attachment and Bowlby's equivalent categories.

Ainsworth	Explanation/description	Bowlby	Description
Securely attached		Securely attached	
Insecurely attached Insecure-avoidant	If the mother consistently rebuffs or rejects the infant's attempts to establish physical contact, the infant may learn to avoid her	Detachment	An active, seemingly defensive disregard for and avoidance of the mother if she returns
Insecurely attached Insecure-ambivalent	Mothers who are slow or inconsistent in responding to their infant's cries or who regularly intrude on or interfere with their infant's desired activities (sometimes to force affection on the infant at a particular moment) produce infants who cry more than usual, explore less than usual (even in the mother's presence), mingle attachment behaviours with overt expressions of anger, and seem generally anxious	Protest	Crying, active searching, and resistance to others' soothing efforts

Table 3.3 Ainsworth's three categories of attachment (with Bowlby's alternative descriptions of the two types of insecure attachment)

Source: Hazen and Shaver (1987, p. 512), adapted with permission

Aim

The aim of the study was to consider whether the three-category theory of attachment could be useful in providing some kind of explanation about romantic love. This led to the formulation of five hypotheses, as follows.

Question 1: Frequencies in the three attachment styles
Can romantic love experiences be categorised in the same way as a child's attachment experiences (as documented by Ainsworth *et al*.)?

The expectation was that it would be reasonable to expect approximately the same proportions as the Campos *et al*. (1983) study (62 per cent secure, 23 per cent anxious-avoidant and 15 per cent anxious-ambivalent).

Question 2: Differences in love experiences
Was Bowlby right when he suggested that the experiences (and therefore attachment relationships) people have with their mothers will result in them experiencing their most important love relationships differently?

The expectation was that:

- *securely attached* people's most important love experience will be characterised by trust, friendship and positive emotions

- *anxious-avoidant* adults' most important love experience will be marked by fear of closeness and lack of trust

- *anxious-ambivalent* adults' most important love experience will be experienced as a preoccupying, almost 'painfully exciting struggle to merge with another person' (Hazen and Shaver 1987, p. 513).

Differences in mental models
The authors were also interested in finding out whether participants had different 'working models' of relationships, as suggested by Bowlby (1969).

Question 3: Attachment history links with romantic attachment styles
Is there a possibility that the different characteristics of parent–child relationships (identified by Ainsworth *et al*.) could explain the adults' mental models and romantic attachment styles?

The expectation was that:

- *securely attached* people will think they are likeable, believe in enduring love and find others trustworthy

- *anxious-avoidant* adults are less likely to believe that romantic love will last and believe that they do not need a love partner in order to be happy; they will also hide any feelings of insecurity

- *anxious-ambivalent* adults often fall in love but have difficulty finding true love; they are more likely to have self-doubts than the other two types because they don't try to repress or hide their feelings.

This was assessed by asking participants if they had ever been separated from the parent for 'what seemed like a long time', whether their parents had divorced and how their parent had behaved towards them as a child (participants were asked to choose adjectives such as responsive, caring, critical, intrusive, etc.).

Question 4: Memories of attachment figures
How do people report memories of their attachment figures (either mother or father)?

The expectation was that:

- *securely attached* people will remember their mother as dependably responsive and caring

- *anxious-avoidant* adults will remember their mother as generally cold and rejecting

- *anxious-ambivalent* adults will remember a mixture of positive and negative experiences with their mother.

Question 5: Vulnerability to loneliness
Are people with insecure attachments likely to have less satisfactory relationships and be vulnerable to loneliness?

The expectation was that:

- *anxious-avoidant* adults will be vulnerable to loneliness, but will try to hide this and report less loneliness than the next type

- *anxious-ambivalent* adults will be vulnerable to loneliness.

Methodology and rationale
In order to answer these questions, two studies were carried out. The first, which served as a kind of pilot study, used participants who replied to a newspaper questionnaire.

The authors were aware that the newspaper sample might have been a self-selected sample (people who were interested in taking part rather than a sample representative of the population as a whole) and so they also decided to test a group of college students studying social psychology (Study 2).

They felt that the first study did not investigate any of the participants' mental models (which might have influenced later relationships), or any investigations into loneliness. In order to remedy this, they included new items intended to address this limitation.

The second study also involved using two more questionnaires to gain more information. The authors found that the two sets of data were very similar and this

Participants
A total of 108 undergraduates (38 men and 70 women) with an average age of 18 years.

Materials
A questionnaire asking participants to describe their most important love relationship, using 56 agree/disagree answers.

A further section was included in order to measure mental models *(by which the authors meant the beliefs the participants held about themselves and others)*. Participants were asked to respond to statements such as those listed below.

- I am easier to get to know than most people.

- I have more self-doubts than most people.

- People are generally well intentioned and good-hearted.

- You have to watch out in dealing with most people; they will hurt, ignore or reject you if it suits their purposes.

A final section measured 'state' and 'trait' loneliness. State loneliness refers to the position the person finds themselves in – that is, whether they are actually physically alone. Trait loneliness relates to the whether they feel lonely, because it is possible to feel lonely even if there are lots of people around.

This was done by asking participants to rate statements and questions on a five-point scale. Examples include:

- During the past few years, I have lacked companionship. *(state loneliness)*

- During the past few years, about how often have you felt lonely? *(trait loneliness)*

Procedure
The students were asked to fill in a questionnaire as a class exercise and data were analysed by number to ensure confidentiality.

Results

Question 1: The results of Q1 identified the participants' attachment types

Attachment type	Prediction	Study 1: newspaper	Study 2: students
Securely attached	62 per cent	56 per cent	56 per cent
Anxious-avoidant	23 per cent	25 per cent	23 per cent
Anxious-ambivalent	15 per cent	19 per cent	20 per cent

Table 3.4 The frequencies identified in the three attachment types

The results supported the prediction that participants would fall into approximately the same proportions as the Campos *et al.* (1983) study. The results of both studies, when averaged, showed that 56 per cent of the participants classified themselves as securely attached, approximately 24 per cent as anxious-avoidant and approximately 20 per cent as anxious/ambivalent.

Question 2: Differences in love experiences

Table 3.5 shows the predictions of the authors about the differences in the love experiences of the participants, together with their actual experiences.

Attachment type	Prediction	Study 1: newspaper	Study 2: students
Securely attached	Characterised by trust, friendship and positive emotions	Especially happy, friendly and trusting (average duration of relationship – 10.02 years; 6 per cent divorce rate)	Friendly, happy and trusting
Anxious-avoidant	Marked by fear of closeness and lack of trust	Experienced fear of intimacy, emotional highs and lows, and jealousy (average duration of relationship – 5.97 years; 12 per cent divorce rate)	Marked by fear of closeness
Anxious-ambivalent	Experienced as a preoccupying, almost 'painfully exciting struggle to merge with another person'	Characterised by obsession, desire for reciprocation and union, emotional highs and lows, and extreme sexual attraction and jealousy (average duration of relationship – 4.86 years; 10 per cent divorce rate)	Marked by jealousy, emotional highs and lows, and a desire for the partner to return the same feelings of love

Table 3.5 The authors' predictions about the love experiences of the participants, together with their actual experiences

Note: The average length of relationship for Study 1 was eight years; the average length of relationship in Study 2 was one year.

The second prediction was that there would be different kinds of love experiences for people in the three attachment-style categories. The results supported the idea that there were three different styles of love rather than three different points on a continuum, although the authors believe that there is a 'core experience of romantic love'.

This hypothesis predicted that the insecure participants would feel more lonely than the secure participants (especially the anxious-ambivalent participants). These results fit with other findings that the anxious-ambivalent adults really want an intense relationship that is all-consuming and probably overpowering. However, they are less likely to find partners to return this level of intense commitment, and are thus more likely to feel 'alone' than the other groups.

Conclusion

The authors suggest that romantic love is a biological process that supports the development of attachments between sexual partners who are likely to become parents. Relationships start with a romantic beginning when the lovers are fascinated and preoccupied with each other. They then move into the period of secure attachment. The relationships that break down can be seen, in part, to mirror the person's previous attachment bonds. They also suggest that 'loneliness and grieving are often signs of the depth of broken attachments'.

Limitations of the study

The authors identify some limitations of the study, but there are other aspects of the study that need to be considered.

- The two groups of participants were not representative of the population as a whole, although the results suggested that the two groups were representative of each other.

- Were all the participants told the purpose of the study and did they give informed consent?

- There were not equal numbers of male and female participants.

- The participants were asked to categorise themselves into one of the three groups by thinking about their love relationship. The question is whether they were able to categorise themselves accurately – they may have chosen the wrong category because they felt one was more socially desirable than the other, or they may just have been very poor at assessing themselves.

- The participants were also classifying themselves by a current relationship rather than their relationship with their parent. Perhaps this resulted in them classifying themselves in a different way, especially if their current relationship was not going well.

- The method used self-report measures. Participants provided information about their relationships with others, which were not checked for accuracy.

- Every relationship we have in our lives is unique and often we have more than one serious love relationship. Perhaps the participants would have given different answers with a different relationship.

APPLICATION OF RESEARCH INTO ATTACHMENT:
Care of Children

Candidates should be able to:
- explain how psychological research relates to care of children – for example, dealing with separation in nurseries, encouraging secure attachments through parenting classes, dealing with stranger anxiety in hospitalised children.

CARE OF CHILDREN

Research into attachment has influenced our knowledge as to the best way of caring for children. For example, we know from Bowlby's research that disruptions in early childhood relationships may have lasting effects on the child's ability to form long and meaningful relationships as an adult. Ainsworth's research has also indicated that the nature of attachment relationships can affect the child's ability to get along with others, their emotional development, their resourcefulness, attention span and confidence in attempting problems.

It is now generally understood that children do need to have a responsive and consistent attachment figure. We also understand from Rutter's research that children can respond to more than one attachment figure, and that it is not necessarily the mother. This has significant implications for the care of children who enter nurseries or who are hospitalised.

Nurseries

It is now much more common for both parents to work, and childcare is a challenge for parents to manage. Therefore many more children attend nurseries than ever before, going from a very young age through to school entry. Although there have been concerns regarding the welfare of children who go to nurseries and the disruption to their attachment relationships, research has shown that if the nursery provides good day care the experience is not harmful and can, in some cases, be beneficial (Lamb 1998).

The selection of a nursery is very important.
- The staff need to be well qualified and sensitive to the children's needs.
- There should be a low staff turnover in order to allow relationships to develop between staff and children, and to provide consistency.
- There should be a high caregiver-to-child ratio (ideally no more than one to four).

Figure 3.5 This baby is using its sensori-motor skills to understand its world

Figure 3.6 The child loses interest in the toy directly it is covered up

From this behaviour Piaget inferred that, by eight months old, the child has developed an internal representation (or image) of the object, which is why it continues to reach for it and show distress that it has disappeared. The baby has therefore achieved object permanence.

Evidence from studies of attachment support Piaget's claim that once the baby develops a mental representation of an object, it understands that it still exists even though it is not seen. Young children demonstrate stranger anxiety at about eight months of age (see page 88). According to the concept of object permanence, they have developed mental representations of the people they are attached to, so that when someone appears who does not match any of those representations, the child shows alarm or fear.

Pre-operational stage (two–seven years)

By two years of age the toddler starts to use symbols, signs or objects to represent things. This is an example of symbolic thinking, which is when we make something 'stand for' something else. For example, the three-year-old will use a cardboard box as a house or a car. Language is evidence of symbolic thinking, because the child knows that when you say 'table' the word 'stands for' an actual table – he could draw one or point one out in the room, or tell you how you could use a table. Piaget said that language skills develop as a result of the child's cognitive development.

Children in the pre-operational stage demonstrate the following characteristics.

● **Animism**: children up to about four years old think that inanimate objects have feelings like they do (this is animism), saying, for example, 'The flowers are tired' when flowers are wilting.
● **Egocentrism**: have you ever played hide and seek with a three-year-old who hides by standing in front of you-covering her eyes? Because she cannot see you, she thinks you cannot see her; this is an example of egocentric thinking (or egocentrism). An egocentric child can see the world only from their point of view, not understanding that other people may have different experiences or may see things differently to them. Egocentric children also focus, or centre, on one aspect of a situation or problem (which helps to explain why young children have difficulty with conservation; see page 118). **Centration** was the term Piaget used for this focus on only one feature.

Piaget and Inhelder (1956) devised the 'three mountains' task to test children's egocentric thinking (see Figure 3.7). For this task, a child sat at a large, table-top model of three mountains and was asked what he could see from his side of the table. A doll was then placed at various positions around the table. The child was shown photographs of the mountains taken from these different positions, and asked to indicate which of them showed the doll's view.

Figure 3.7 The task for the child is to describe the view of the mountains that the doll has. For example, the correct answer would be that the nearest mountain is the one with the house on.

Four- and five-year-old children thought the doll's view would be the same as their own, which indicates egocentrism. However, most seven-year-olds identified the doll's view correctly, which suggests that their thinking is no longer egocentric.

Conservation

During this stage, children are unable to conserve number, length, quantity, mass, weight and volume. Their understanding is dominated by the appearance of something and so they do not understand that a quantity of something will remain the same when it is presented in

Conservation	Method	Apparatus
Number	Two rows of equal numbers of counters, laid out in parallel with the items matching. The child is asked 'Are there the same number of counters?' One row is stretched or rearranged, and again the child is asked 'Are there the same number of counters?'	
Mass	Two identical pieces of clay are shown to the child (1). 'Is there the same amount of clay in each?' One is rolled out into a sausage shape (2) and the child is asked 'Is there the same amount of clay in each?'	
Volume	Two equal-sized glasses have the same amount of liquid in each. The child is then asked 'Is there the same amount of liquid in each?' The liquid from one is poured into a taller glass. The child is then asked again 'Is there the same amount of liquid in each?'	

Table 3.8 Studies of conservation of number, mass and volume: an overview

a different way. Piaget undertook a series of experiments to test children of different ages' ability to conserve (described in detail in the core study for this chapter, page 130). Table 3.8 offers a brief description of studies that have looked at the conservation of number, mass and volume.

Children's responses to each of these tests would have been focused on the appearance of the objects, so the answer to the second question in each conservation experiment would have been 'No'.

Concrete operational stage (seven–11 years)

Early in the concrete operational stage the child starts to be able to de-centre, which means that they are able to understand that people see things differently from them.

- They would be able to identify the doll's view in the three mountains task.
- They understand that objects can belong to more than one class – for example, they would be able to think of their mother as a mother and as an aunt.
- They are also able to conserve – they can now understand that something is the same, even though its appearance changes. Conservation develops slowly but in the same order, with conservation of number appearing by about seven years of age, then mass and length between seven and eight, then weight between the ages of eight and ten, and finally volume by 11 to 12. However, the children in this stage need to have the actual objects present in order to complete the task (which is why it is called the concrete operational stage).

Formal operational stage (11 years and older)

The child in the previous stage could manipulate things, but in the formal operational stage the child can manipulate ideas. A simple example is the ability to envisage relationships, as in the following problem:

- If Mark is taller than Ali, and Mark is smaller than Kerry, who is the tallest?

In the previous stage the child would have to draw a picture or use different-sized objects to solve this problem. Now the child can manipulate the ideas in her/his head. It can do mathematical calculations, think creatively, imagine the outcome of particular actions.

According to Piaget, once the young person has achieved formal operational thinking, there is no further change in the structure of thinking, only in the complexity, flexibility and level of abstraction.

about various skills such as how to mix colours in art, how to cook or how to behave in different situations, without having to find out for themselves. This cultural knowledge can be handed on without the child having to learn by trial and error. The child can then, in turn, hand the same skills on to the next generation.

Zone of proximal development

Vygotsky identified the importance of social influence on children's development by explaining that adults provide **scaffolding** to help them learn. He believed that children are able to demonstrate certain abilities on their own, but with help and guidance from others, they can actually achieve more. This help and guidance, or scaffolding, may start off being really directive, but can slowly be withdrawn as the child becomes more capable and manages to do things or reason out complex problems on her or his own.

The difference between a child's independent achievements and their potential achievements is called the **zone of proximal development**. The people who can help and guide them do not have to be adults – they could even be other children who are more capable. As Vygotsky says:

> The zone of proximal development … is the distance between the actual developmental level as determined by independent problem solving and the level of potential development as determined through problem solving under adult guidance or in collaboration with more capable peers. (Vygotsky 1978, p. 86)

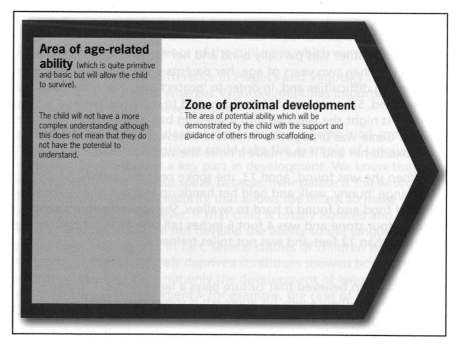

Area of age-related ability (which is quite primitive and basic but will allow the child to survive).

The child will not have a more complex understanding although this does not mean that they do not have the potential to understand.

Zone of proximal development
The area of potential ability which will be demonstrated by the child with the support and guidance of others through scaffolding.

Figure 3.9 The area of overall ability that is made up of age-related ability plus the zone of proximal development; the zone will vary according to the ability of the child, with 'brighter' children having larger zones

Once the child has received the advice and guidance from the adult, they will internalise the knowledge with practice. Take, for example, a child who is given a box of bricks. The child will play with the bricks, may lay them out or sort them for colour. They may find that, by putting one on top of the other, they can make a tower. However, if an adult or older child is there with them and shows them how to make a tower, they are likely to copy and learn the properties of the bricks more quickly. This example illustrates how the scaffolding provided by social interaction with the adult will give the child the chance to achieve more.

We have already identified how important social relationships are in other areas of children's development when we looked at attachment relationships in the earlier part of this chapter. Vygotsky, through his theory, highlights the importance of social relationships in learning. Because his theory focuses far more on the *opportunities* a child has to learn and experience, it is not age related in the same way as Piaget's. Although he believes that children do go through developmental stages in a uniform order, Vygotsky is more flexible in the way that he looks at development.

INTRODUCTION TO THE CORE STUDY

Piaget's book, *The Child's Conception of Number* (1952), which was first published in Switzerland in 1941 as *La Genèse du Nombre chez l'Enfant*, contains ten chapters that look at different aspects of the way children learn about numbers, and how their developmental stage dictates their understanding. The majority of children who were involved in the studies that make up this book were all in the pre-operational stage of development (aged between four and eight years).

The core study covered here is found in Chapter 4 of Piaget's book; however, to put the study in context, we are going to consider Chapter 3 and the beginning of Chapter 4.

Chapters 1 and 2 consider the child's ability to conserve quantity, and Piaget investigates this using methods such as the conservation of liquid experiment (outlined earlier in this chapter, page 118). From these studies he identified different stages of conservation ability.

Chapter 3

Piaget begins Chapter 3 by explaining that correspondence means 'looking at the relationship between two quantities'. This can either be done by comparing their size (e.g. length) or by making what he describes as a 'one–one' correspondence between the elements, that is, by saying whether two sets of objects are equal in number. Sometimes it is quite difficult to compare two sets of objects because they may look very different due to the way they are set out. (See Figure 3.10, which might make this easier to understand although it is not included in Piaget's book.)

offer feedback to the pupils when necessary. Pupils would also engage in group learning or peer mentoring (working with another pupil who may be more able or older). Pupils should also be taught how to use cultural 'tools' such as computers, books, and graphs as a way of supporting their learning and presentation (Anita Woolfolk 2004). This would allow the pupils to internalise the new information and use it in the future, and to progress at a faster pace than if they were left to their own devices.

CHAPTER 4

Social psychology

We are all social beings, and relationships have been shown to be one of the most important things in our lives. Research has shown that if humans are deprived of other human company for prolonged periods, they may start to hallucinate or have vivid dreams about other people. Because social relationships and social interactions are so essential to our well-being, this has resulted in a branch of psychology that focuses on understanding our social behaviour. Social psychologists are interested in looking at the ways our behaviour is influenced by **social context**, and the ways in which we are able to communicate our feelings without using words.

- The first section of this chapter gives some insight into the research that has been conducted to explain obedience, and the core study tries to find an explanation as to why we are more likely to carry out a task if we are asked by someone in a uniform.
- The second section focuses on non-verbal communication, considering its function and how it develops. Non-verbal communication varies between cultures and the core study focuses on the fact that some cultures view parts of the face as being more significant than others.

acceptable. In order to check this out, the study was replicated in a tatty, downtown office block and it was found that the obedience levels dropped a little but were still 48 per cent.

When the researcher gave up his grey laboratory coat and simply looked like a member of the public, the level of obedience fell to 20 per cent. This indicates that his 'uniform' must have had some influence on obedience levels.

Culture

By culture, we mean a set of shared attitudes, values, practices and goals, which are found in different races, in institutions, organisations and groups. If the majority of members of a culture share these 'norms and values', most people would find it very difficult not to conform to the group norms. Research into conformity has indicated how an individual will go along with the group, even when they know that the answer is wrong.

One of the most famous pieces of research into conformity was conducted by Solomon E. Asch (1951). He devised a series of laboratory experiments with groups of six to nine people who were seated round a table. There was one participant, but the rest were confederates (they were pretending to be participants), who had been told to give the wrong answers on certain trials. Asch said he was testing visual perception and showed the group lines of different lengths (see Figure 4.2). Each person said whether line A, B or C was the same length as the test line. All the confederates would give an incorrect answer (for example, saying the test line was the same length as line A). When the participant was asked to give his answer, in 25 per cent of cases he would conform to the rest of the group, even though when the participants were tested alone, there were very few wrong answers.

The participants who gave the answer given by the rest of the group did so because they felt discomfort at being 'the odd one out', even though the majority later explained that they knew they were giving the wrong answer.

Overall, 75 per cent of participants conformed to the wrong answer at least once. The average rate of conformity was 32 per cent.

Now imagine, if you found yourself in a similar situation where everyone holds a certain opinion or behaves in a certain way, it would be very difficult to stand up and actively go against the majority. In fact, many of the repressive regimes in the world have developed a culture of obedience that serves to control the population. Conforming to cultural norms does not have to involve the threat of punishment. It is threat enough to feel that you might be rejected by the majority if you do not go along with these norms. If the culture sees compliance as a normal way of behaving, then we

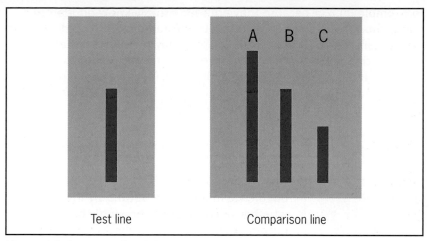

Figure 4.2 An example of the test line and the comparison lines in an Asch experiment.

would expect higher levels of obedience. If, on the other hand, the culture favours individuality and challenge, obedience would probably be lower.

A different procedure was used in research by W. Meeus and Q. Raaijmakers (1986) in the Netherlands. They required participants to criticise a 'candidate' (actually a confederate) whom they were 'interviewing' for an important job. Here 92 per cent obeyed instructions, delivering the most insulting comments.

Although we accept that culture affects conformity *and* obedience, it is difficult to make direct comparisons between studies that have taken place in different countries. When experimental procedures are different, this may account for differences in results rather than differences in culture.

THE EFFECT OF AUTHORITY AND THE POWER TO PUNISH ON OBEDIENCE

Considerable research has gone into looking at what we mean by authority and what makes an effective authority figure. For example, John R.P. French Jr and Bertram Raven (1959, 1969), who are mentioned in the core study, developed their Social Power Theory, which looks at the six bases of social power (see page 158). They suggest that people get power from a number of sources, from the ability to reward

Figure 4.3 Russian soldiers marching during a Victory Day Parade on Red Square in Moscow. How difficult would it be for one of them to disobey? They would have to actively defy their commanders and go against the consensus of the regiment in a culture of obedience to higher authority; the result would most certainly be unthinkable

(e.g. employers) or because they are seen as very knowledgeable about the subject and people respect their judgement (e.g. doctors on health), and so on. One source of power they mention is what they call 'coercive power', which comes from having the ability to punish the person if they disobey or are actively defiant. We can immediately think of a number of examples of this kind of authority figure, from the teacher, to the policeman, to the army commander.

HOFLING *ET AL.*'S HOSPITAL RESEARCH

ASTROTEN

5 mg capsules
Usual dose: 5 mg
Maximum daily
dose: 10 mg

Figure 4.4 This is the label the nurses saw in the ward medicine cabinet

Hofling and colleagues (1966) studied obedience in a real-life setting by investigating whether nurses would knowingly break hospital rules in order to obey a doctor. The authority and power a doctor had in a hospital in 1966 would have meant that it was extremely difficult for the nurse to challenge the doctor's authority, and she would have been fearful of losing her job should she refuse to obey his commands.

A bottle of pills had been labelled 'Astroten' and placed in the ward medicine cabinet (see Figure 4.4).

The nurse on duty received a phone call from a Dr Smith from the Psychiatric Department, asking her to give his patient 20 mg of Astroten straight away. He explained that he was in a hurry and wanted the drug to have taken effect before he got to see the patient, and that he would sign the drug authorisation when he came on the ward in about ten minutes' time.

These instructions broke the following hospital rules:

● nurses give drugs only after written authorisation
● nurses take instructions only from people they know
● maximum dosages should not be exceeded.

Nevertheless, 21 of the 22 nurses phoned by 'Dr Smith' obeyed the instructions, although someone stopped them from actually administering the drug, which was a harmless sugar pill. When interviewed afterwards, many nurses said that doctors frequently phoned instructions and became annoyed if the nurse protested. Half the nurses said they had not noticed what the maximum dosage was. The researchers described the situation to a **control group** of 21 nurses and then asked what they would have done. Each claimed that they would not have obeyed. This suggests that the unequal power between doctors and nurses, rather than the knowledge of correct procedure, affected the nurses' behaviour.

Philip Zimbardo's prison simulation experiment

We know from Milgram's work that different settings influence people's behaviour and may make them behave in a way that is different from normal. We have also seen from Hofling *et al.*'s work that the fear of punishment makes people more likely to obey. Imagine a situation where a perceived legitimate authority figure gave permission (and actually encouraged) a group of students to act in a harsh and authoritarian way towards another group of students, demanding that they obey often unreasonable demands.

One of perhaps the most famous pieces of psychological research used exactly that scenario. Zimbardo (1971) recruited 22 male students from newspaper advertisements to take part in a study of prison life. All the participants were screened to make sure that they were stable, mature and had no antisocial tendencies. They were then randomly allocated to the role of 'prisoner' or 'guard'.

A basement corridor in Stanford University was converted into a mock prison containing three small cells, a solitary confinement area, a recreation 'yard', and several rooms nearby for the guards. The 'prisoners' were given a uniform of loose-fitting smocks with identification numbers, a nylon stocking on their heads to cover their hair, no underwear, and a lock and chain around the ankle. This process of **deindividuation** removed any sort of individuality they had. They had already signed a consent document, which specified that some of their human rights would be suspended, and they were told that they must remain in the prison for the duration of the study. The 'guards', who had also been given a military-style khaki uniform, reflective sunglasses, clubs, whistles, handcuffs and keys, were told they could not use physical violence although they were expected to 'maintain a reasonable degree of order' within the prison.

The 'prisoners' were arrested by the police (as part of the study, although they did not know this was going to happen) and went through the usual procedure for prisoners before being put in their cells. The activities in the 'prison' were carefully recorded including using video and audio tape. However the experiment had to be stopped after six days, principally because of the pathological reactions of the participants.

Figure 4.5 A participant in Zimbardo's prison simulation experiment

The guards became absorbed in what has been described as the 'pathology of power', where they enjoyed the power they felt they had been given. Their first orders to the prisoners involved getting up in the middle of the night for roll call, or doing press-ups. The prisoners tried to assert their independence over the guards, rebelling. The guards continued to respond, with their aggressive behaviour becoming more extreme over the week, treating the rebels to a fire extinguisher, taking their clothes from them, preventing them going to the toilet, removing their mattresses, and so on.

The prisoners became more and more despondent and obedient as the days went by. The experiment was terminated after six days due to their extreme response. Remember, they had done nothing wrong and had just been randomly allocated their roles. Why did they not continue to rebel? Why did they ultimately comply to the guards' commands? The reason was that they had been made to feel that they were helpless and fearful. The social power the guards demonstrated had made them obedient and unwilling to challenge this perceived authority.

At first glance, this experiment seems quite simple in its outcome – that the power the guards held over the prisoners made the guards behave in the way they did, and resulted in the obedience of the prisoners. However, the results may actually be more complex. Zimbardo suggests that the guards *were* certainly conforming to the way they believed guards should behave. In other words, it was not bad people doing bad things but ordinary people acting out a part that was created for them by the situation they were in. This is a controversial view, not least because it doesn't even describe what happened in Zimbardo's experiment. The Stanford Prison Experiment had a prison superintendent who controlled the whole procedure and set the standards for the guards. That superintendent was Zimbardo. In his opening speech to the guards at the start of the experiment he said:

> They will have no freedom of action. They will be able to do nothing and say nothing we don't permit. We're going to take away their individuality in various ways... We have total power in the situation. They have none. (Zimbardo 2007, p. 55)

Notice the use of pronouns here. Zimbardo puts himself with the guards and gives clear instructions that 'we' are going to go outside normal patterns of social behaviour to create a hostile situation for the prisoners. It is not, as Zimbardo suggests, that the guards wrote their own scripts on the blank canvas of the experiment, but Zimbardo himself created the script of terror. What we also see in this study is the obedience of the guards to the tyranny created by the superintendent (rather than simply the obedience of the prisoners).

One last thought – it is important to realise that the problem with coercive power is that the individual will not necessarily internalise the behaviour, so as soon as the authority figure is out of sight they may well do what they want. Hofling *et al.*'s nurses would have refused to give the incorrect dose if it had been up to them.

Zimbardo's guards would have been more compassionate without Zimbardo, and the prisoners would not have chosen to get up in the night or lose their mattresses if the guards had not been present.

THE EFFECT OF CONSENSUS ON OBEDIENCE

If we have been given a command and we are not sure whether we should obey, or even if it is the right thing to do, we may well look and see what others are doing as a way of deciding if it is the correct course of action. If the consensus of opinion – that is, the widespread agreement among all members of the group – is to do as we have been told, this consensus will affect our obedience.

In a situation like this, we will usually feel more comfortable about the decision we have made (even if it is wrong) because of what is known as '**diffusion of responsibility**'. Here is an example of how this works. You are on your own in a library and you are 'playing' on a computer. The program has sound and you are wearing headphones but they are quite uncomfortable. Because there is no one around, not even the librarian, you unplug the headphones and carry on. Suddenly the librarian comes storming in and shouts at you to turn the music off. Reluctantly, you do so. Now imagine the same situation if there were two of you – the librarian's anger would not seem so bad. Now imagine there were 15 of you and you all decide to have the music playing. The reprimand would be much less personal and unpleasant because the responsibility would be shared by all of you, and you might even choose to ignore it. The obedience you would have shown when on your own has totally changed because of the presence of the other people.

Consensus of opinion (and therefore diffusion of responsibility) can be very powerful in changing the behaviour of others who would, under different circumstances, act very differently. One example of a real-life situation which could perhaps be explained by this phenomenon was the massacre at My Lai during the Vietnam War. The commanding officer ordered his soldiers to kill everyone in a village (even though there were only women, old men and children). The consensus of opinion of soldiers is that their commander is legitimate and therefore must be obeyed. They consequently followed his commands. Lieutenant William Calley, the commanding officer, had been told the enemy were hiding in the village. He was later court-martialled, claiming he was 'only following orders'. One of the soldiers at Calley's trial explained:

> Lieutenant Calley told me to start shooting. So I started shooting. I poured about four clips into the group... They were begging and

saying, 'No, No.' And the mothers were hugging their children and ... well, we kept right on firing. They were waving their arms and begging ... (*Life* 67(23), 5 December 1969)

There is another explanation for these horrific events, however. The suggestion that comes from conformity research and from Zimbardo's study is that the people running the death camps or the people at My Lai were just ordinary men in extraordinary situations, but is this so? What if they specifically sought out those jobs or sought out a murderous regiment in the US Army? Perhaps there was something about their personality. The evidence gives more support to this argument than to the 'ordinary men' explanation.

CRITICISMS OF SITUATIONAL FACTORS AS AN EXPLANATION OF OBEDIENCE

There are some criticisms of the research evidence that has been used to support the idea that situational factors are an explanation of obedience. These criticisms focus not only on the research itself, but also suggest that there may be other reasons why we are obedient.

Although Milgram's research suggested that environmental factors can influence people's willingness to obey, additional studies indicate that this cannot be the only reason, because when he replicated his study in a downtown office block, people still obeyed the orders of the experimenter to a much higher level than would be expected. Perhaps this was to do with the personality of the experimenter rather than the situation itself!

Milgram also saw that people were more likely to muster the courage to defy an authority figure when they saw someone else do so. When participants were one of three 'teachers' and the others refused to give the shock, Milgram found that obedience dropped to 10 per cent. Several said afterwards that they had not realised they could refuse to continue.

Milgram found that if his participants took personal responsibility for the suffering of the learner, such as putting the learner's hand on the electric plate, obedience dropped to 30 per cent. Perhaps the fact that they were unable to deny what was going on meant that their personal values were more important than the environmental pressures.

Much of the research that considers the impact of the situation on levels of obedience tends to ignore our personal cognitions. We are brought up in a society that supports a hierarchical structure of power, and we learn from an early age that to do as you are told is the correct way to behave. This is reinforced through school and by the rule of law. We actually find it quite difficult to disobey.

Therefore when we are faced with a command that we want to defy, this causes us to feel a high level of anxiety and discomfort because we are going against what we have always learned. This discomfort is known as **cognitive dissonance** (discomfort with our cognitions or thought processes). Therefore we are more likely to obey than to actively challenge because it makes us feel much more comfortable (**cognitive consonance**).

When we obey someone else, we are putting the responsibility for the actions on them. In fact we are acting as an agent for the other person rather than acting according to our own values and conscience. Milgram (1973) described these different states of mind as agentic and autonomous, where an agentic state means people suppress their own values, no longer feeling responsible, and an autonomous state is when they act according to their own values and conscience.

Hofling *et al.*'s (1966) research (see page 150), indicating that the nurses in a hospital setting were blindly obedient to an authority figure with the power to punish, was challenged in research by Steven G. Rank and Cardell K. Jacobson (1977) using a similar procedure. However, this time the drug was Valium®, which was a familiar drug to all the nurses. Here only two of the 18 nurses obeyed the instructions, the researchers concluding that familiarity with the drug was one reason for the low level of obedience in their study. Therefore it was not the situation that dictated obedience because the nurses chose to defy the doctors as they knew the request was dangerous. They may have felt cognitive dissonance when refusing, but they introduced the third belief – the doctor is wrong – to allow them to defy the command.

DISPOSITIONAL FACTORS AS AN ALTERNATIVE THEORY OF OBEDIENCE

Do you think that the situation can always explain why someone is obedient? Do you think, from what we have said so far, that there might be something about the person obeying that makes them more likely to do as they are told than another person? Could it be that they have a distinct personality type, so the explanation is to do with their **disposition** rather than the situation?

It is very likely that you have been in a group where you have been told to do something, and some of the people you are with will blindly agree and do exactly as they were told while others will just rebel and refuse. The ones that agree seem to be very willing to conform, so even when the request is unreasonable they would say things like 'We have to do it; we have been told to.'

This kind of person might be described as an authoritarian personality, a type that was identified by Theodor W. Adorno *et al.* in 1950.

Adorno and his colleagues were trying to explain the conditions that allowed anti-Semitism (prejudice towards Jewish people) to take hold in Nazi Germany. They were interested (as was Milgram) in whether there was something about the German population that was different because, otherwise, why did the German nation not challenge the mass murder of the Jews? They used various psychological scales to try to identify why some people are more susceptible to **fascism** and authoritarian belief systems than others, thinking that this might be the explanation they were looking for.

Once the data had been collated, Adorno *et al.*'s work was published in 1950 in a book called *The Authoritarian Personality*, which caused outrage among some members of the population. The book contained the Adorno F-scale, which consisted of a list of statements that would be scored on a six-point scale (see Table 4.1), and was the tool Adorno *et al.* devised to measure fascist (F) tendencies. Their suggestion was that some members of the German population had higher F scores than other groups.

According to Adorno, the authoritarian personality shows the following characteristics:

● excessive conformity
● submissiveness to authority
● intolerance of others who are different
● insecurity
● superstition
● rigid, stereotyped thought patterns.

These characteristics make someone with an authoritarian personality subservient to people of higher status, and actually quite hostile to people they consider to be inferior. They are suspicious of people who have different values and ways of life to what they consider to be the norm, and are unwilling to look for alternative opinions and views. Perhaps these were the people who responded to Zimbardo's advertisement. Perhaps they were the kind of people who signed up to fight in the US Army.

Figure 4.6 Nazi soldiers interviewing Jewish people during the Second World War

According to Adorno *et al.*, the authoritarian personality has its roots in Freud's psychoanalytic theory, which indicates that early childhood experiences affect the development of personality. In Chapter 1 we talked about psychoanalytic theory and gender roles. Psychoanalytic theory suggests that young boys internalise the values of their fathers as they experience the Oedipus complex. Therefore if you have a very strict, highly authoritarian father, this means you may well develop very strong internalised

Obedience and respect for authority are the most important virtues children should learn.					
A person who has bad manners, habits and breeding can hardly expect to get along with decent people.					
The business man and the manufacturer are much more important to society than the artist and the professor.					
Every person should have complete faith in some supernatural power whose decisions he obeys without question.					
What the youth needs most is strict discipline, rugged determination, and the will to work and fight for family and country.					
An insult to our honour should always be punished.					
Sex crimes, such as rape and attacks on children, deserve more than mere imprisonment; such criminals ought to be publicly whipped, or worse.					
Most of our social problems would be solved if we could somehow get rid of the immoral, crooked and feebleminded people.					
Homosexuals are hardly better than criminals and ought to be severely punished.					
Most people don't realise how much our lives are controlled by plots hatched in secret places.					
Disagree strongly 1	Disagree mostly 2	Disagree somewhat 3	Agree somewhat 4	Agree mostly 5	Agree strongly 6

Table 4.1 A sample of the statements from the F-test, together with the scoring system

male characteristics, which will be based on your father's values. If the father is very strict and authoritarian, the child will also become strict and authoritarian. Freud also suggested that we repress some of our desires and drives that are not considered acceptable. However, these have to surface in some way, so they are projected on to minority groups who are different to us, and this is the basis of prejudice and discrimination.

CORE STUDY: Bickman (1974)

Bickman, L. (1974) The social power of a uniform. Journal of Applied Social Psychology *4, pp. 47–61.*

Candidates should be able to:

- describe Bickman's field experiment into the effects of uniform

- outline the limitations of Bickman's study.

Background

A person's appearance will affect whether people obey them or not. One of the things that might influence compliance is the person's clothes, because if they are wearing a uniform we may be more willing to obey them than if they are wearing casual clothes. The type of uniform will also affect how we respond and whether we feel the command is legitimate. After all, we are more likely to obey a policeman than a postman, even though they both wear uniforms. Bickman points out that, throughout history, uniforms have been important in signifying power. He also mentions that dress can indicate social class or lifestyle, affects people's honesty, their helping behaviour and can actually have an effect on the wearer himself.

The author also talks about what is known as Social Power Theory. French and Raven (1959, 1969) categorised the basis of social power. They suggest that people get power from the following means.

- Reward power: people believing that the person who is in power has something they want and so they will obey for that reason.

- Coercive power: if they don't obey, the person in power will be able to punish them.

- Legitimate power: the person is perceived as having some sort of legitimate power, such as a car park attendant in a car park, a bouncer in a nightclub or a teacher in a classroom.

- Referent power: the person is perceived as attractive to the person who is willing to comply.

- Expert power: the person possesses superior knowledge or ability.

- Informational power: the person knows more than everyone else.

Some types of power are only effective with surveillance, such as coercive power (*this is why people often speed when there is no likelihood of being seen by the police*),* and reward power (*you have to be seen to do something in order to get the reward*). The other types are not based on surveillance, so people would obey whether or not someone was watching them.

* Text in italics was not reported in the actual study.

The aim of this study is to measure the degree of social power that someone has if they are wearing a uniform, and to try and find out which of French and Raven's categories could be used to explain this power. They suggest that sometimes power is effective only in certain situations, and cite the example of a doctor being able to get us to undress in a surgery but not in a public place.

In order to look at all the aspects of power, French and Raven conducted four experiments.

Experiment 1

Aim

The aim was to see if a person wearing a uniform but acting out of role still has more power than a person without a uniform using 'out-of-role' behaviour.

- Experiment 1 was designed to find out whether a man dressed as a uniformed guard will have more ability to influence individuals than when he is dressed in a low-authority uniform (milkman) or in his normal clothes.

- Experiment 2 was designed to investigate the basis of this social power.

Method
Field experiment.

Participants (Ps)
An opportunity sample of 153 adult pedestrians walking along a street in Brooklyn, New York. (People were selected if they were between the ages of 18 and 61, were alone and had not witnessed the previous participants' interactions with the experimenter.)

The average age of Ps was estimated (in five-year intervals) by the experimenter and an observer to be 39 years of age; 43 per cent were male and 57 per cent female.

Procedure
There were four experimenters (Es). One acted as a confederate (helper), the other three were dressed as noted in Table 4.2.

Uniform	Clothes	Level of authority
Civilian	Sports jacket and tie	Lowest level of authority
Milkman	White coat, carrying a basket full of empty milk bottles	A little authority
Guard	Looked like a policeman but with a different badge	Highest level of authority

Table 4.2 Clothes worn by three of the experimenters

All Es were white males, between 18 and 20 years of age. All wore the same-size suits and all were of similar build. All followed the same procedure without knowing the purpose of the experiment. The experiment was conducted during weekdays.

Each experimenter followed each procedure. The procedures were as follows.

- Paper bag: the E stopped the P and asked them to 'Pick up this bag for me!' If the P did not do it immediately, the E would explain he had a bad back. P was considered to have obeyed if he picked up the bag.

- Dime: E stopped the P, pointed to a confederate standing beside a parked car at a parking meter, and said 'This fellow is over-parked at the meter but doesn't have any change. Give him a dime!' If the P did not do it immediately, the E would explain he had no change either. P was considered to have obeyed if he gave the confederate a dime or made an effort to find change by searching for it.

- Bus stop: if P was standing alone at a bus stop, the E would approach and say 'Don't you know you have to stand on the other side of the pole?' The sign says 'No Standing' (this actually meant that cars weren't allowed to wait in the bus stop area). If P did not do it immediately, E would say 'Then the bus won't stop here, it's a new law.'

If the Ps did not do as they were asked, even after the explanation, the Es left.

Results
The following table shows the number and percentage of Ps who obeyed.

Uniform	Situation						Average % over 3 situations
	Paper bag		Dime		Bus stop		
	N	%	N	%	N	%	
Civilian	14	36	24	33	15	20	19
Milkman	14	64	14	57	14	21	14
Guard	22	82	20	89	16	56	38

Table 4.3 Obedience results for each individual trial, and the total results for all three situations

The author points out that, in every **condition** (situation), the Ps were more obedient to the higher authority figure (guard). There was no statistically significant difference between the Ps' obedience to the civilian and the milkman, so any difference that was seen was just due to chance *(which could have been due to something as simple as the mood of the people on the day rather than the outfit of the Es).*

Looking at the average percentage of obedience by outfit rather than simply by situation, the guards had the highest score, while the milkman had the lowest score.

- 25 per cent of Ps did what the E asked without any further explanation.
- 36 per cent of Ps did what the E asked following the explanation.
- 39 per cent of Ps did not do what the E asked.

There was no difference in the number of men or women who helped. Age made no difference either.

The author made a number of comments about the results, as follows.

- The research was intended to measure obedience to a demand, but some Ps may have thought it was simply a request for help, especially those that heard the explanation (and even more so in the paper bag condition).
- Many Ps were surprised when they were stopped.
- The author speculated as to whether the explanation provided by the Es affected the Ps' behaviour. He suggested that it might have given Ps time to think about the request, or indicated that the request really was serious.
- Ps were less willing to obey in the bus stop situation. Perhaps the reason for this was because this was the only situation when the P was not asked to do something for someone else who was needy. The command was based on an untruth and most people in New York would know that the sign referred to cars, not people waiting for a bus.

The author explains that coercive power may be the reason why people obeyed the guard. If he was thought to be some sort of law enforcement agent, he could be considered a threat to the Ps.

The author then suggests that if the guard's power really is based on either reward or coercion, then surveillance will be an important factor in whether or not people comply *(remember – you are less likely to speed if the police are watching you)*. This leads him to Experiment 2, which was intended to look at the basis of this social power.

Experiment 2

Aim
The aim of Experiment 2 is to see whether the guard's power is affected by surveillance.

Participants
Forty-eight adult pedestrians in Brooklyn, New York, average age 46 (Ps selected and 'aged' in the same way as the Ps in Experiment 1); 60 per cent were male and 40 per cent female.

Procedure

In this study, the guard and the civilian were used, plus one confederate. They were all white males aged between 20 and 24. All were similar in build. The Es enacted the parking meter scene.

- Surveillance condition: the procedure was the same as Experiment 1 except the Es waited a little longer if the Ps did not comply, before giving an explanation.

- Non-surveillance condition: both Es went through the procedure as follows. The E (walking away from the meter) approached the P (walking towards the meter). At a point about 50 feet from the parking meter the E stepped into the P's path saying 'You see that guy over there by the meter [pointing]. He's over-parked but doesn't have any change. Give him a dime!' By the time the P reached the confederate, the E had gone round a corner and was no longer in sight (so the P wasn't being observed). The P was not given any explanation.

Results and discussion

Uniform	Condition				
	Surveillance		Non-surveillance %		Total % who obeyed in both conditions
	No. of Ps obeying (total no.=12)	%	No. of Ps obeying (total no.=12)	%	
Civilian	6	50	5	42	46
Guard	9	75	11	92	83

Table 4.4 Percentage of Ps obeying for each uniform under surveillance and non-surveillance conditions in Experiment 2; also total who obeyed in both conditions

The results replicated those found in Experiment 1. In only 25 per cent of cases was the explanation given.

- Guard: all Ps responded positively in some way to the guard (e.g. by saying something positive or nodding their heads).

- Civilian: seven Ps tried to ignore the civilian.

The results showed that surveillance had no effect on compliance. This led the author to conclude that the results could therefore not be explained by either reward or coercive power, which is thought to be effective only if there is also surveillance. The author then wondered whether the Ps believed the power of the guard was legitimate power (even though the situations used did not suggest that the guard would have legitimate power).

Experiment 3a: Perceived legitimacy

Aim
The aim of Experiment 3a was to find out if legitimate power could explain Ps' willingness to comply.

Participants
A total of 141 college students (no information given as to how they were selected).

Materials and procedure
Questionnaires containing a description of *either* a young man, milkman or guard stopping someone on the street and telling them to do something, were randomly distributed to the Ps. There were 29 situations described, including the three from Experiment 1. Ps were asked to say how reasonable these requests were on a ten-point scale where 1 was very legitimate and 10 was not legitimate at all.

Results and discussion
The results indicated that the Ps did not rate either the civilian, milkman or guard as more legitimate in any of the three situations used in Experiment 1.

Of the remaining 26 situations, eight provided significant results with participants saying that the uniformed guard making these requests was not legitimate, and therefore the request was unreasonable. (Perhaps the Ps felt that he was abusing his uniform to try to get people to obey him.) These situations included being asked to smile, sing a tune, deliver a package, laugh, mail a letter, tie the Es' shoes and carry a package.

Experiment 3b: Predicting behaviour
The author then decided to ask Ps what they and others would do in different situations. He explained that if the social power was based on legitimacy *(e.g. a policeman, who is seen in society as being a legitimate authority figure)* then people will be more likely to comply.

Aim
The aim of this part of the study was to see if people were more likely to say they would obey a legitimate authority figure.

Participants
A total of 189 different college students (again no details were given as to how they were selected).

Method and procedure
The Ps were randomly given a questionnaire describing the bag, dime or bus stop situations with either the civilian, milkman or guard giving the order. They were asked

depend on the situation. The author also suggested that the uniformed guard's power could be explained as legitimate power in certain situations.

Limitations of Bickman's study

Many of the limitations of Bickman's study relate to the methodology used. For example, we are not told how the college students were recruited to take part in the research; this might suggest that they might not have been willingly recruited and might not have taken the research seriously. Would it be possible to compare the results from the students with the people on the street, who were considerably older?

With regard to the Ps who were involved in the field study on the streets of New York, they did not give their consent and we could argue that this was not really ethical, although the results would have been affected if they knew in advance the purpose of the research.

The Ps' ages were estimated by the researchers and these estimates may not have been accurate. However, the results are unlikely to have been affected by mistaken ages.

Although the researchers suggested that the only Ps who took part were those who had not seen any previous trials, they could not be sure that the Ps had not walked past earlier and seen what was going on.

The Es were all young, white males. This may have affected the Ps' responses as some might have felt intimidated or uncomfortable because of their characteristics.

The experiments were conducted at different times. Experiment 1 was carried out in the week, while Experiment 2 was carried out at the weekend. This may have resulted in two different types of Ps (perhaps unemployed people during the week and employed people who were shopping at the weekend). Therefore, were the results comparable?

Finally, do you feel that the questionnaires were as useful as the field experiments in collecting realistic data?

APPLICATION OF RESEARCH INTO OBEDIENCE: keeping order in institutions and situations

Candidates should be able to:
- explain how psychological research relates to keeping order in institutions, e.g. the use of punishment in schools, use of authority in armed forces, effect of prison setting.

KEEPING ORDER IN INSTITUTIONS AND SITUATIONS

Obedience theory has highlighted that the nature of the situation, the culture and the personality of the individual all impact on how it is possible to maintain order in our institutions. The situation itself may dictate the kinds of behaviours that are expected, and we learn how to play the role that is required, either by experience or by instruction. For example, schools require pupils to maintain order, to attend lessons, to be polite, to be quiet in class and to study hard. Members of the armed forces also have carefully prescribed roles that require compliance and obedience at all times in order to do their duty. The role of the prisoner is to follow the instructions of the guards, to come and go as dictated by the prison regime, and to serve their time.

We do know that many people who have been subjected to high levels of control rarely internalise and adopt the behaviours they have been made to demonstrate, and this must be remembered when considering how to keep control in institutions.

Use of punishment in schools

Schools have expectations as to how the pupils should behave. In fact, if you speak to the older generations, they may well recall when physical punishment was used in schools to keep order. The slipper, the ruler and the cane were all used as a form of corporal punishment for misdemeanours. Behaviour was less challenging within the school environment, and this has been one of the arguments to suggest that we should continue to use punishment as a way of maintaining order. Today, corporal punishment is forbidden, so the punishments provided, such as removal from class, removal of privileges, detentions and exclusions, it could be argued, are less frightening.

However, behaviour theory suggests that punishment is not effective as a way of helping children to learn the correct way to behave. The theory behind punishment is that all behaviour, except the required behaviour, is punished as a way of shaping the required behaviour. However, unless the child knows what the required behaviour actually is, how can they possibly know what they should be doing?

Children are expected to obey school rules and behave in a way that allows them to learn. For the majority of pupils, this is not a problem, as they have parents who value education and who will actively support their progress through school. On the other hand, there are others for whom education has no value, as their role models and experiences lead them to expect little from their world. They may well understand the consequences of breaking school rules, but if they do not value what school has to offer, then why should they conform?

THE ROLE OF REINFORCEMENT AND PUNISHMENT IN LEARNING NON-VERBAL BEHAVIOUR

Learning theory, which we will talk about in more detail in the next chapter, has indicated that we are likely to repeat a behaviour if it is rewarded (or reinforced). On the other hand, behaviour that is punished, by which we mean behaviour that results in something unpleasant happening, is less likely to appear again (see Chapter 5, page 203). It would make sense to think of non-verbal behaviours being learned in the same way. Imagine a young child watching a couple of adults shaking hands with each other. The child who imitates this behaviour by offering their hand, would receive a warm response from the adult concerned, who is likely to be enchanted by the behaviour and will smile and react positively to the child. This response will act as a positive reinforcement and so the child will have learned that shaking hands as a greeting is a good behaviour to demonstrate. Similarly, imagine the case of a small child watching his father's aggressive or intimidating stance towards another person who then backs down. This child may well then produce a similar behaviour in the playground as a way of intimidating other children and their response of fear might act as a positive reinforcement, making it more likely that this behaviour will appear again.

You may well have provided a 'punishment' response to a non-verbal behaviour in the past. Imagine the experience of being with someone who stands just a little too close, to the extent where it makes you feel uncomfortable. You will find yourself backing away to make the distance between you feel more comfortable. If they keep on invading your personal space, you may decide that you find it *too* uncomfortable to be with them. Similarly, if someone you don't know very well keeps touching you or wanting to stroke you or play with your hair, this behaviour would not be appropriate and you will probably avoid them in the future. They would probably get the same response from others and this response to their behaviour would act as a kind of punishment. We would hope that they would learn that this is not the behaviour to exhibit.

One piece of research evidence illustrated how the responses of adults help to shape young people's understanding of personal space. Personal space is like a bubble that surrounds us and keeps people at bay. When people invade that space by standing too close, we feel very uncomfortable and will try to move away. A.M. Fry and F.N. Willis (1971) conducted a survey which showed that people expect children to have learned appropriate personal distance by the age of ten. They therefore organised for children aged five, eight and ten to stand six inches behind adults in theatre queues. The results showed that the five-year-olds got a positive response, the eight-year-olds were ignored and the ten-year-old children were given a cold reaction. The response to the behaviour of the ten-year-old children was quite negative, and would have made them feel uncomfortable and less likely to produce the same behaviour again.

CULTURAL VARIATIONS IN NON-VERBAL COMMUNICATION

Because there are cultural variations in non-verbal language, this supports the idea that we learn culture-specific behaviour through socialisation (nurture), otherwise we would all behave in exactly the same way. You may have seen the film *Borat*, which tells the story of the fictitious character Borat Sagdiyev, who comes from Kazakhstan, portrayed by the actor Sacha Baron Cohen. The film is the story of Borat's journey across America and features a series of episodes when he interacts with members of an unsuspecting public who had no idea that he was acting and really believed in his fictitious character. The film, which was nominated for several awards, demonstrates what happens when someone breaks many of society's taboos and behavioural norms. The film is extremely funny in parts but also makes the viewer cringe with embarrassment as 'Borat' does things that are totally unacceptable in America. The film also demonstrates how important it is for us to understand that different countries have different expectations as to how we should behave.

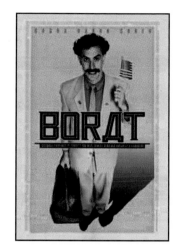

Table 4.9 gives examples of the different non-verbal behaviours that are seen in different parts of the world. It is not a complete list, but will give you an idea of how behaviours that we may take for granted are actually unacceptable in other cultures.

CRITICISMS OF THE SOCIAL LEARNING THEORY OF NON-VERBAL BEHAVIOUR

We have shown that many non-verbal behaviours are learned, as they vary from culture to culture. However, there are some universal non-verbal behaviours that seem to be common to all cultures and are displayed from birth – in other words, they are genetically controlled rather than learned by observation (for example, smiling). We will talk more about these types of behaviours in the next section, which looks at evolutionary theory as a way of explaining non-verbal behaviours.

The main criticism of the social learning theory of non-verbal behaviour comes from the fact that it cannot be used to explain some of the more complex behaviours that we, as human beings, display. You will probably have realised that some of our bodily communication is spontaneous and some is under our cognitive slouching. Although you may have copied these behaviours initially, you will learn not to do them and to do something different by direct command, rather than learning what to do by observation alone.

EVOLUTIONARY THEORY

So far, we have shown that a number of non-verbal behaviours are learned by observation, although sometimes our bodily responses override the behaviour we would like to produce. We have also discussed the way that certain non-verbal communications are demonstrated across all cultures, and this indicates that they may not actually be learned but may instead be something we have genetically inherited from our ancestors. In fact, if we consider evolutionary theory as a way of explaining non-verbal communication, we can see that many of these behaviours are linked to survival rather than simply being associated with cultural norms.

Charles Darwin, in his book *The Expression of the Emotions in Man and Animals* (1972), suggested that the primary emotions conveyed by facial expressions are universal. By that he meant that all humans everywhere express and interpret these facial expressions in the same way. He gave the example of how we will wrinkle our noses if we smell something horrid, or smile to show that we want to be friendly. He believed that facial expressions have a kind of evolutionary significance and a survival value. This would make sense because the universal nose-wrinkling expression would convey to anyone that something (smell or taste) is unpleasant and therefore should be avoided, the smile suggests that you are not going to attack and therefore should not be attacked in return, and so on.

Evidence to show that the six major emotional expressions (anger, sadness, happiness, surprise, fear, disgust/contempt) are universally understood came from one study by P. Ekman and W.V. Friesen (1971). They went to a remote tribe in New Guinea where they told members of the tribe short stories with emotional content. They showed them photographs of American men and women expressing these six emotions and asked them to pick the photograph that went with the story. They were very accurate in their ability to pick the right photograph.

The reason why this universal ability to understand non-verbal communication is especially important is because of the role it plays in the two most important evolutionary functions: surviving and reproducing. In order to survive, we need to protect our territory and our food. If we are to reproduce, we need to somehow communicate to our possible mate that we are interested in them in a sexual way.

Much of the evidence for the significance of non-verbal behaviours comes from **comparative psychology** – that is, looking at animal

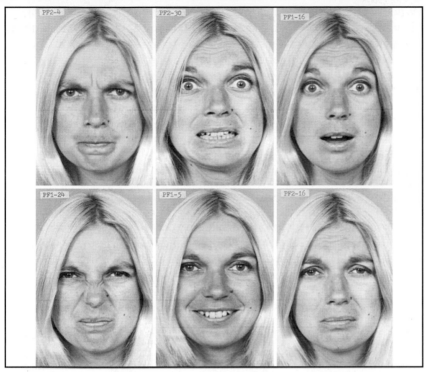

Figure 4.11 Photographs used in some of Ekman and Friesen's research, showing anger, fear, surprise, disgust/contempt, happiness and sadness

behaviour as a way of understanding human behaviour. If we accept the theory of evolution, it would make sense to think of humans as being at the top of the evolutionary hierarchy. However, because we are still animals, we are nevertheless likely to demonstrate the same sorts of behaviours as other animals. The trouble is, it is quite difficult to observe and assess human behaviour as we are so good at hiding our motives, so if we really want to understand the function of non-verbal behaviours, it makes sense to look at other animals who are less likely to be affected by someone observing them.

Survival

In order to survive, animals will need to warn off others and this involves demonstrating aggression. Animals show their aggression by baring their teeth, by curling their noses or by 'squaring up' to an opponent. Rarely do animals fight to the death. What they do is to signify their hostility by using a series of ritualised behaviours to pass that message on to their potential opponent. This is often seen in domestic dogs, who will give off warning signals before actually fighting with a rival for your affections (or their dinner). These non-verbal responses serve the function of conveying aggression without the potential consequences.

Human beings also demonstrate very similar aggressive behaviours. They might 'square up' to a possible opponent, stare at them, flaring their nostrils, and possibly even invading their personal space. This is usually enough to warn another human being not to come any closer. These ritualised aggressive non-verbal behaviours have been identified by Peter Marsh, Elizabeth Rosser and Rom Harré (1978), who undertook a longitudinal study of Oxford United football fans by videoing and interviewing them over time. They discovered that their aggressive behaviour towards opposing fans was also ritualised and their gestures and postures, although seen as aggressive, rarely resulted in any sort of physical conflict.

Reproduction

If an animal wants to reproduce, they first of all have to attract a mate. In the animal kingdom, mating displays are often very complex and colourful, with the male of the species doing their best to attract an available passing female (see Figures 4.12–4.14).

Figure 4.12 The bower bird signifies his desire for a female by building this elaborate 'house'

Figure 4.13 The albatross engages in a long courtship dance

Humans also have a series of non-verbal behaviours that are intended to attract the attention of a member of the opposite sex. These may involve wearing certain clothes, body posture, tone of voice, prolonged eye contact, pouting lips, swaying motion when walking, and so on. By using non-verbal communication, it is possible to communicate intentions without asking a direct question. This way, if the other person is not interested, they can simply pass by without causing either party any direct embarrassment.

It might be possible to argue that many of our behaviours are learned; a better argument is that we inherit certain non-verbal behaviours through genetics, but that our socialisation will moderate the behaviour itself in order to make it socially acceptable.

Figure 4.14 This peacock is displaying his splendid tail to a passing peahen, to attract her attention

Figure 4.15 The girls in this picture are showing their interest in the boys by their posture; similarly the boys are maintaining their gaze and posing in response

CORE STUDY: Yuki *et al.* (2007)

Yuki, M., Maddux, W.W. and Masuda, T. (2007) Are the windows to the soul the same in the East and West? Cultural differences in using the eyes and mouth as cues to recognise emotions in Japan and the United States. Journal of Experimental Social Psychology *43, Elsevier, pp. 303–311.*

Candidates should be able to:

- describe Yuki *et al.*'s experiment into cross-cultural differences in interpreting facial expressions

- outline the limitations of Yuki *et al.*'s study.

Introduction

Facial expressions are our primary means of communicating emotions, so it is important that we can interpret the facial expressions of others.

Research evidence suggests that facial expressions of basic emotions can be generally recognised, but more recent research has shown that people from different cultures interpret facial expressions differently (Hillary Anger Elfenbein *et al.* 2004). We are more accurate in judging the emotional expressions of people who are from our own cultural group or a group that we are familiar with. The reason for this might be because there are facial 'dialects' or 'accents' in people's expressions that are understood by the people who belong to that particular group and that they use on a regular basis.

So far, past research has not managed to identify these 'accents', so the authors proposed that facial cues from different parts of the face take on more significance

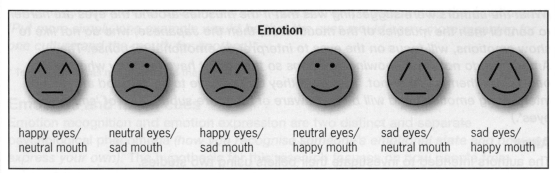

Figure 4.16 The emoticons used for the first study
Source: Yuli *et al.* (2007), reproduced with permission

Participants

A total of 118 American students (33 male and 85 female) at Ohio State University and 95 Japanese students (72 male and 21 female, two gender undisclosed) at Hokkaido University took part.

Participants volunteered to take part in the experiment to earn partial course credit in an introductory psychology class.

Procedure

Participants were asked to say how happy or sad each emoticon looked on a nine-point scale (1 = extremely sad, 9 = extremely happy). The participants were then debriefed and thanked for their time.

Results

Happiness

The results showed that the Japanese rated the emoticons as happier when happy emotion showed in the eyes, whereas Americans rated the emoticons as happier when the happy emotion showed in the mouth.

The Japanese also rated the happy eye emoticons as happier than did the Americans, who rated the happier mouth faces as happier than did the Japanese.

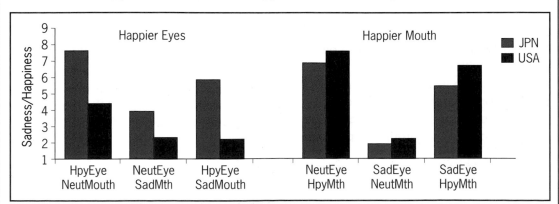

Figure 4.17 The results of the research (Study 1)
Source: Yuki *et al.* (2007), reproduced with permission

Figure 4.17 is taken from Study 1 and shows the results of the research. The Japanese participants clearly focus more on the eyes when judging happy emotions.

Neutral
For the emoticons including happy and neutral cues, results showed that the Japanese perceived the emoticon with happy eyes/neutral mouth as happier than did the Americans. The Americans rated the emoticon with the neutral eyes/happy mouth as happier than did the Japanese.

For the emoticons with sad and neutral cues, results also showed that the Americans rated the emoticon with the neutral eyes/sad mouth as sadder than did the Japanese. However, the Japanese rated the emoticon with sad eyes/neutral mouth only slightly sadder than did the Americans.

Mixed
The Japanese perceived the happy eyes/sad mouth emoticon as happier than did the Americans, whereas the Americans perceived the sad eyes/happy mouth emoticon as happier than did the Japanese,

Discussion
Results from Study 1 supported the authors' predictions. The Japanese participants focused more on the eye expressions, while the Americans gave more interpretive weight to the mouth when rating emotions. The hypothesis was most strongly supported with the mixed emoticons, and supported the prediction that the Japanese participants would use the eyes as a major cue while the Americans focused more on the mouths.

The authors note that Japanese and Americans tend to use different types of emoticons in computer communication, and point out that perhaps the Americans are not as familiar with the 'happy eye' expression (^^). On the other hand, the Japanese had no problems interpreting the mouth expressions. In order to get over these cultural differences in the use of emoticons, a second study was suggested, using the expressions in the faces of real people.

Study 2
Method
A questionnaire was used to gather information.

Materials
Photographs were selected from *Pictures of Facial Affect* (P. Ekman 1976), a set of facial expressions that had been shown to be universally recognisable and reliable expressions of specific emotions. Computer software was used to create faces with the same combinations of mouths and eyes as were used in Study 1. There were 60 faces created from ten different people – each person providing one set of six photographs.

The resulting faces formed ten lots of six combinations that were used in Study 1.

slightly sadder but there was no difference in the second study). They suggest that all cultures may find a particular part of the face to be more important than another part in showing certain emotions *(e.g. if you saw someone crying and sobbing, no matter what culture you come from, you would be pretty sure the person was upset).*

- They suggest that future research could present participants with just the top or bottom half of a face rather than putting them together in an artificial way.

The implications for the current research might explain why Japanese are often said to be 'expressionless or inscrutable'. It is not that they are expressionless, just that they show their emotions through their eyes alone but that westerners miss these cues. The Japanese may also be better than the Americans at detecting 'false smiles' or even if someone is lying.

The authors suggest that the results help to explain why the emoticons are different between Japan and the United States, where one uses variations in the eyes and the other in the mouth, although these differences might be due to the limitations of texting.

The authors conclude with the following points.

- Are the findings generalisable to other cultures who could be categorised as interdependent or independent, besides the Japanese and Americans?

- Will the same cultural differences exist for other emotions, such as fear, anger, surprise and disgust?

- Did the rating scales restrict the responses of the participants? Perhaps they would have preferred to provide a description of the face rather than having to say the face looked either happy or sad.

- Japanese and Americans may just be less sensitive to the eyes or mouth as emotional cues rather than both being sensitive but weighting them differently.

- Social context may also impact on the interpretation of emotions *(which is why we have to be careful when interpreting crying – it may mean tears of joy, depending on the context).*

Limitations of Yuki *et al.*'s study.

The following limitations were identified by the authors in their general discussion.

The original photographs, which had been pre-validated, were actually of the whole face (not just eyes or mouth). When the photos where broken down into parts, perhaps they lost their validity (suggesting that the only way they were valid was if they were seen as wholes). Then, when they were reassembled, they became quite bizarre. The authors point out that the face involving happy eyes and a neutral mouth results in an overall expression that looks like a kind of scowl. The authors do state that they felt that the photos served the purpose of this particular study, which was the interpretation of emotions from eyes and mouth, rather than overall expressions of emotions. However, we cannot be sure if the authors were correct.

Were photographs or emoticons an effective way of illustrating facial expressions of emotions? Do you think that this method lacked 'ecological validity'?

Figure 4.19 shows an example of how facial parts convey less emotion than the whole face. What emotion does each picture convey? Could you put these together and, if so, would you find it easier to identify the emotion?

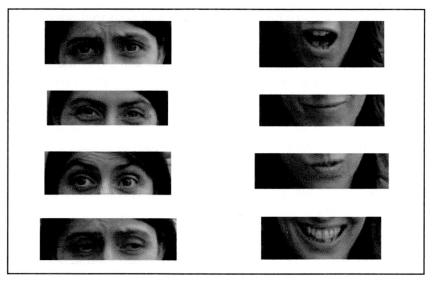

Figure 4.19 An example of how facial parts convey less emotion than the whole face

The rating scales may have affected the results. For example, if you were asked to say whether a face looked happy or sad, you may say it did not look happy or sad, but actually looked confused or annoyed. However, that option is not available to you so your results would not really indicate what you believe.

The sample, which consisted of students who were gaining points towards a first-year course, is not representative of the population as a whole. They were a self-selecting sample who may also have lacked motivation to take the whole study seriously. The authors do not state whether the students completed the questionnaires alone or in groups so they may have copied each other's answers.

Individual differences

The psychology of individual differences helps us to understand that although we belong to the species known as human beings, in many ways we are actually very different to each other. It is important for psychologists to help identify both these similarities and differences in order to further the understanding of how we live and operate in our world.

- The first section of this chapter considers how we learn and how, with some of us, that learning can become distorted and develop into a kind of mental disorder known as a phobia. The study for this section looks at how it is possible to create a phobia in a child.
- The second section looks at the differing beliefs psychologists hold – either that we are unique and therefore cannot be measured and compared to each other, or the alternative belief that we actually have many aspects of our personality in common and so can be compared. The core study focuses on how owning pets can affect the way we feel about ourselves and also highlights some of the techniques used to measure personality.

Psychoanalytic theory suggests that our behaviour is caused by unconscious forces. These unconscious forces, according to Freud, shape a person's personality, which is made up of three parts, as follows.

1. The **id** contains the instinctive sexual and aggressive energies that we are born with, and these instincts are buried in our unconscious. When a need arises we are driven to satisfy it immediately.
2. The **ego** starts developing at around three years old, as we begin to understand that we cannot always have what we want and must satisfy our needs in realistic ways. For example, we cannot show our true feelings towards our parents.
3. The **superego** develops at around six years of age and is the moral part of our personality, which is also in the unconscious.

The role of the ego is to mediate the conflict between the urgent demands of the selfish id and the restraints of the superego. We are not aware of this conflict because it occurs in the unconscious, but we *are* aware of the anxiety it creates. For example, if a child was frightened of a parent, the id would say 'run away'. The ego must handle this anxiety by trying to prevent the child from fleeing, but if the anxiety is so great that it threatens to overwhelm the ego, we protect it by using **ego defence mechanisms**. Three that relate to phobias are those described below.

1. **Repression** – in which we force memories of distress or conflict into our unconscious, where they remain unresolved. If we find ourselves in a similar situation, the same feelings re-emerge.
2. **Displacement** – in which we transfer our negative feelings (such as fear) away from the cause of the feelings and on to something that will not harm us. For example, a psychoanalytic explanation for xenophobia (fear of foreigners) could be that an individual hated

his father and was frightened of him. He was unable to express these feelings towards the father, and so **displaced** them on to foreigners. The individual feels able to express his feelings towards foreigners in a way that he cannot towards his father.

3. **Projection** – in which unacceptable feelings are attributed to someone else. The xenophobic man who hated his father (and unconsciously wanted to harm him) might **project** these feelings on to foreigners. He sees foreigners as wanting to harm him and is therefore fearful of them.

Freudian theory can help to explain the powerful emotions experienced by phobics. It can also help to explain why the phobic is fearful of objects or situations with which she or he has no direct experience. However, because conflicts are in the unconscious, they are not accessible, so it is not possible to be sure that these are the causes of phobias.

EVOLUTIONARY THEORY AS AN ALTERNATIVE THEORY TO EXPLAIN PHOBIAS

Evolutionary theory can provide an alternative explanation to phobias. If we ask the question why are people more likely to develop a phobia of spiders than, for example, cars (which are much more dangerous), is it that there is an innate element to such fears? M.E.P. Seligman (1971) proposed that our ancestors were threatened by many dangers, and being sensitive to these dangers would increase their chance of survival – as a result, we have evolved the ability to associate certain stimuli with danger and this ability (or preparedness) explains phobias to things (snakes) or situations (heights), which may be dangerous.

Some of the best human laboratory evidence for biological preparedness has come from comparing the conditioning of participants to 'natural' items such as spiders and snakes rather than man-made but nevertheless potentially dangerous items such as weapons and electricity outlets. Participants were wired up to receive electric shocks every time they saw specific photographs, in order to make the association between specific items and pain. The participants were more easily conditioned to respond with fear to the 'natural' items and the effects were much more long-lasting (G.C.L. Davey 1995).

The core study for this section looks at the development of a phobia in a very young boy. It illustrates how, through the process of classical conditioning, 'Little Albert' developed a phobic fear of white furry things.

3. Dog alone. Turned away but did not fall over. Cried. Hands moved as far away from the animal as possible. Whimpered as long as the dog was present.

4. Rat alone. Slight negative reaction.

5. Rat and sound. It was thought best to freshen the reaction to the rat. The sound was given just as the rat was presented. Albert jumped violently but did not cry.

6. Rat alone. At first he did not show any negative reaction. When rat was placed nearer he began to show negative reaction by drawing back his body, raising his hands, whimpering, etc.

7. Blocks. Played with them immediately.

8. Rat alone. Pronounced withdrawal of body and whimpering.

9. Blocks. Played with them as before.

10. Rabbit alone. Pronounced reaction. Whimpered with arms held high, fell over backward and had to be caught.

11. Dog alone. At first the dog did not produce the pronounced reaction. The hands were held high over the head, breathing was checked, but there was no crying. Just at this moment the dog, which had not barked before, barked three times loudly when only about six inches from the baby's face. Albert immediately fell over and broke into a wail that continued until the dog was removed. The sudden barking of the hitherto quiet dog produced a marked fear response in the adult observers!

The conclusion was that poor Albert's fear was so great that it didn't matter where he was. Watson and Rayner suggested that these results indicated that 'emotional transfers do take place', and they suggested that the same fear response may well occur in a large number of different places.

Question III: The effect of time upon conditioned emotional responses
Watson and Rayner wanted to see how long the conditioned response lasted but Albert left the hospital a month after the previous tests. During the remaining month, he was not subjected to any more 'conditioning' experiences although he was brought into the laboratory for other tests on his general development.

Age one year 21 days – Santa Claus mask, fur coat, rat, rabbit, dog

1. Santa Claus mask. Withdrawal, gurgling, then slapped at it without touching. When his hand was forced to touch it, he whimpered and cried. His hand was forced to touch it two more times. He whimpered and cried on both tests. He finally cried at the mere visual stimulus of the mask.

2. Fur coat. Wrinkled his nose and withdrew both hands, drew back his whole body

and began to whimper as the coat was put nearer. Again there was the strife between withdrawal and the tendency to manipulate. Reached tentatively with left hand but drew back before contact had been made. In moving his body to one side his hand accidentally touched the coat. He began to cry at once, nodding his head in a very peculiar manner (this reaction was an entirely new one). Both hands were withdrawn as far as possible from the coat. The coat [p. 11] was then laid on his lap and he continued nodding his head and whimpering, withdrawing his body as far as possible, pushing the while at the coat with his feet but never touching it with his hands.

3. Fur coat. The coat was taken out of his sight and presented again at the end of a minute. He began immediately to fret, withdrawing his body and nodding his head as before.

4. Blocks. He began to play with them as usual.

5. The rat. He allowed the rat to crawl towards him without withdrawing. He sat very still and fixated it intently. Rat then touched his hand. Albert withdrew it immediately, then leaned back as far as possible but did not cry. When the rat was placed on his arm he withdrew his body and began to fret, nodding his head. The rat was then allowed to crawl against his chest. He first began to fret and then covered his eyes with both hands.

6. Blocks. Reaction normal.

7. The rabbit. The animal was placed directly in front of him. It was very quiet. Albert showed no avoiding reactions at first. After a few seconds he puckered up his face, began to nod his head and to look intently at the experimenter. He next began to push the rabbit away with his feet, withdrawing his body at the same time. Then as the rabbit came nearer he began pulling his feet away, nodding his head, and wailing 'da da'. After about a minute he reached out tentatively and slowly and touched the rabbit's ear with his right hand, finally manipulating it. The rabbit was again placed in his lap. Again he began to fret and withdrew his hands. He reached out tentatively with his left hand and touched the animal, shuddered and withdrew the whole body. The experimenter then took hold of his left hand and laid it on the rabbit's back. Albert immediately withdrew his hand and began to suck his thumb. Again the rabbit was laid in his lap. He began to cry, covering his face with both hands. [p. 12]

8. Dog. The dog was very active. Albert fixated it intensely for a few seconds, sitting very still. He began to cry but did not fall over backwards as on his last contact with the dog. When the dog was pushed closer to him he at first sat motionless, then began to cry, putting both hands over his face.

The authors concluded that their experiments showed that not only directly conditioned responses but also transferred responses continued for over a year, although they did note that Albert's response was not as intense. This suggests that conditioned responses may persist, adapt or modify over a human's lifetime. The authors did acknowledge that Albert was 'an extremely phlegmatic type', by which they meant he was a placid baby. If he was more highly strung and emotionally unstable, his responses would probably have remained as strong as they were originally.

Question IV: 'Detachment' or removal of conditioned emotional responses
The authors were unable to investigate how to remove Albert's conditioned emotional responses because he was taken away from the hospital on the day the previous tests were carried out. They did suggest that any conditioned emotional responses that came from the home were likely to continue unless they were accidentally 'deconditioned', but for the ongoing unpleasant conditioned responses, it was important to work out a specific way of effectively removing them in order to ease the suffering of the affected person.

Watson and Rayner suggested that they might have tried the following techniques:

- regularly showing the child the stimulus so they became used to it and the reflex response would die out

- by trying to 'recondition' the response by showing the child the objects they feared and at the same time stroking them

- by trying to 'recondition' by feeding the child sweets or other foods at the same time as they saw the object they feared

- by showing the child how the object was not scary so that they could imitate the adult's behaviour (e.g. stroking/touching it) or by holding the child's hand to stroke/touch it.

Incidental observations

Watson and Rayner made some additional observations during their experiments:

- Albert sucked his thumb as a way of managing his fear and rage. When they tried to film his fear responses, they had to remove his thumb before he reacted so it seemed that the thumb sucking blocked his fear response. Other children who had been restrained during Watson and Rayner's experiments would stop being upset if they had something to suck (e.g. a finger).

Watson and Rayner concluded their report by suggesting that if 20 years later Albert was still afraid of fur and hair, he might approach a Freudian therapist. The trouble is, the analysis of his fear would probably miss the point. The Freudian therapist might ask him to recall a dream and this dream would be interpreted to give an explanation of the basis of the fear. The story might go along the following lines: Albert, when he was about three years of age, tried to play with his mother's pubic hair. He would have been severely told off for this behaviour (thus pairing the hair with the unpleasant stimulus), and this would have been the basis of his avoiding tendencies. Albert might therefore feel that this is the true basis of his phobia.

Watson and Rayner suggested that many of the phobias people experience are conditioned emotional reactions (either direct or transferred) and the people who experience phobias may well be 'constitutionally inferior', by which they meant lacking in strength and confidence. However, it is important to remember that emotional disturbances may have developed from not only love, but also from fear and rage.

Limitations of Watson and Rayner's study

As with all case studies, Watson and Rayner's study investigated the development of a phobia in one child and, by their own admission, this child was particularly placid. Therefore the results may not be generalisable to the population as a whole.

When people develop phobic responses, they are often unaware of where these have come from, but it would certainly not be from a laboratory setting. Therefore it might be possible to argue that this experimental study lacks ecological validity.

At the time of this research, ethical guidelines as we know them today did not exist. However, if you read the description of poor Albert and his growing fear of fur and hair, it is hard to imagine how his mother could have agreed to let him go through this level of discomfort. Were Watson and Rayner honest about the nature and process of their research? Did Mrs B give informed consent to Albert taking part?

Another ethical consideration is that any participant in psychological research should not be harmed in any way. Although it would seem, from Watson and Rayner's account, that Albert did not suffer long-term lasting damage, it is for certain that he did not leave the research environment in the same psychological state as he was in when he entered. The authors were also unable to desensitise him as his mother withdrew him from their experiment.

Watson and Rayner did suggest, however, that they were concerned about Albert's welfare:

> At first there was considerable hesitation upon our part in making the attempt to set up fear reactions experimentally. A certain responsibility attaches to such a procedure. We decided finally to make the attempt, comforting ourselves by the reflection that such attachments would arise anyway as soon as the child left the sheltered environment of the nursery for the rough and tumble of the home. We did not begin this work until Albert was eleven months, three days of age. (p. 4)

The justification that he would develop other fear responses allowed them to continue. As Richard Gross (1999) points out, was 'he likely to have encountered any of the other stimuli while his ears were assaulted by the sound of a full-grown man striking a hammer upon a large steel bar immediately behind his head?' (p. 305).

APPLICATION OF RESEARCH INTO ATYPICAL BEHAVIOUR: BEHAVIOUR THERAPY FOR PHOBIAS

Candidates should be able to:
● explain how research relates to psychological behaviour therapy for phobias, e.g. use of stimuli, systematic desensitisation, use of classical conditioning in flooding and implosion therapy, cognitive therapy for going beyond behaviour modification.

BEHAVIOUR THERAPY FOR PHOBIAS

Although we cannot explain every atypical behaviour by using behaviourist theory, it seems that some of the most successful treatments of phobias have relied on behaviourist principles, which suggests that they are simply the result of maladaptive learning. Therefore behaviourists would argue that the best way to treat phobias is to re-educate the sufferer.

Use of stimuli

In order to help an individual get over a phobia they have to, at some point, be exposed to the thing they most fear. Imagine someone who is terrified of spiders being told that they will have to have one crawling over their hand in order to realise that spiders really aren't that scary. They might get so distressed by the thought of the spider that they will refuse to go through any sort of therapeutic intervention. However, at some point they will have to be exposed to the spider in order to know that they have been 'cured'.

Therapists often use different stimuli to help the process, using photographs, film and model objects, say, to begin the process, as these are thought to be less frightening.

Systematic desensitisation

The principle behind systematic desensitisation is to replace the client's feeling of fear with another, very different sensation. The new sensation is one of deep relaxation, with the aim being that, on exposure to the feared object, the client will suddenly feel very relaxed rather than very frightened. In effect, the client is going through a process of **counter-conditioning** – a new process of conditioning to counteract the previous one.

The client will be asked to construct a list of the most frightening things they can imagine in relation to their phobia and to put it in a hierarchy, with the most feared situation being at the top and the least frightening thing being at the bottom of the list. The top of the list might be for the client to imagine being shut in a coffin with hundreds of spiders of different sizes. The bottom might simply be a picture of a friendly spider in a children's book. The therapist might use different stimuli, such as model spiders or films of spiders, to help the client with their hierarchical list.

Once the client has been taught deep relaxation techniques, whereby they imagine every muscle in their body losing any sort of tension or stress, then the process of systematically desensitising them will begin. The therapist will get them to relax, and will ask them to think about the least frightening thing on their hierarchy. Once they can do this with no anxiety, they will then think of the next one on the list. This process will happen over a series of sessions until the client is able to imagine the most fearful situation without feeling any degree of anxiety at all.

Flooding and implosion therapy

Behaviour therapists suggest that classical conditioning is the cause of phobias. Because the client has made the association between the object and an unpleasant event, they are extremely fearful and will avoid the object at any cost. This means that they will never challenge their fear. Therefore the answer is to make them challenge this unfounded fear by exposing them to the feared object, as quickly and extremely as necessary.

The difference between flooding and implosion is as follows.

- Flooding means to expose them to the actual object rather than any more neutral stimuli. With a spider phobic this might involve throwing a bucket of spiders all over them, or, with someone with agoraphobia, it might be to deposit them in the middle of a desert. The idea is that they will be very frightened, but the body cannot maintain that level of arousal for any length of time because it becomes exhausted. The level of fear cannot go any higher and so it will have to come down; with this, the person will realise that the feared object is not so scary after all.
- Implosion uses the same technique but instead of the person being exposed to the actual object, they will be exposed to the thing they imagine would be the most horrific (the item that came top of the list in the process of systematic desensitisation).

Cognitive therapy

We have already mentioned that people are actually quite complex, with complex thoughts and feelings that are sometimes disordered and therefore incorrect. Certainly this might be the case with people who experience phobic responses to specific things – after all, why should anyone be irrationally fearful of the number eight (octophobia), because there is no obviously logical reason for this fear?

A great deal of our behaviour occurs as a result of our thoughts. We think, this affects how we feel, and this dictates the action. Supposing we think we need a new outfit to go to a party as we think all our clothes look awful, we will feel that we need to go and get a new outfit or we aren't going, and therefore we will go shopping. If we think we are not liked by a group of people, we will feel unliked and will therefore avoid them and stay at home. These thoughts may not actually reflect the truth of the situation. They are simply our belief system. The idea behind cognitive therapy is to address these thought processes and help the person to develop a different way of looking at things that will in turn affect their behaviour.

In Figure 5.3, the negative thought affects the way the person feels and this in turn will affect what they do, which will reinforce their initial thought.

If we link this with treatment for phobias, we might ask a person to engage in something like systematic desensitisation, but the person may be thinking as they go through the process that they have not actually been exposed to the offending item itself, which is *still* really dangerous. They will still be feeling anxious and scared. In fact, they might go through the process of desensitisation feeling that they are doing it because they have been pressurised into it. Because of this, their thoughts will not have changed and these thoughts are more likely to dictate their future behaviour than anything else. Therefore the only way that any treatment would be effective would be to change the thoughts themselves.

Cognitive behavioural therapy (CBT) relies on challenging negative, automatic thoughts and replacing them with different thoughts. If we take the example of a fear of spiders, the following conversation shows how, by challenging these thoughts, the person will reassess their beliefs.

Negative automatic thought: Spiders are horrible scary things that will bite me and I might die.

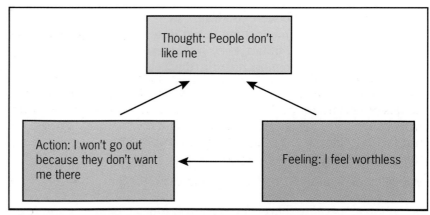

Figure 5.3 How negative thoughts are reinforced

Question: What is your evidence?

Answer: Well, people do get bitten by spiders.

Question: How many people do you know about who have been bitten and then died?

Answer: Lots of people in Australia have been bitten by spiders and I expect lots of them have died.

Question: What is your evidence?

Answer: Well, er, um.

Question: According to the BBC Health News in 2004, only 26 deaths from spiders have been recorded in Australia in the past century. No deaths have been recorded from spider bites in the UK. How likely do you think it is that you will die from a spider bite?

Answer: Not very likely.

Question: What is your evidence?

Answer: No one in the UK has ever died of a spider bite.

Question: Do you know anyone who has ever been bitten by a spider?

Answer: No.

Question: What is your evidence?

Answer: If they had they would have told me.

Question: How many times have you been bitten by a spider?

Answer: Never.

Question: How likely do you think it is that you will be bitten by a spider?

Answer: Not very likely.

Question: What is your evidence?

Answer: Because neither I or my friends have ever been bitten by a spider.

What is happening here is that the therapist is challenging the negative automatic thought and making the client think about their beliefs. By asking for evidence to support the disordered or incorrect train of thought, the client will begin to see how their arguments are not factually based. This will make them feel very different about things, and this should then impact on their behaviour.

We will look again at CBT in the second part of this chapter, page 243.

THE SELF

OVERVIEW

In the first part of this chapter, we talked about how our individual experiences can have an influence on the way that we react to different situations. Because of this, and because we don't all have the same experiences, people do not always act predictably. Psychologists, therefore, tend to look at how the majority behave in any given situation, and make predictions from that information.

KEY CONCEPTS

The OCR examination requires candidates to be able to:

- understand the idea that individuals are unique
- explain the concept of free will.

THE SELF

Some psychologists do not feel that we should group people into categories. They say that it is essential that we look at each person as being unique, with their own set of hopes and fears for the future. This does make sense when you consider how no two people have the same experiences.

The factors that go towards making humans unique are as follows:

- family position – first born, middle child, youngest
- gender – boy or girl
- family structure – one parent, two-parent family, step-siblings, grandparents, etc.
- parenting style – harsh or too easy-going
- social class and educational opportunities
- cognitive ability – level of intelligence
- any sort of learning difficulty – e.g. dyslexia
- any sort of physical disability – e.g. hearing impairment
- physical appearance – height, weight, hair colour

- personality – introvert (likes being quiet and prefers the company of one or two to a crowd) or extravert (outgoing sociable type who likes noise and lots of people)
- life experiences – where you live, type of school, type of teacher
- religious beliefs
- culture and ethnicity.

If we consider for a moment all the factors that make humans unique, by considering the list above, you will probably understand why, even from the same family, no two children are going to be the same. Although they may share genes and family structure, they will still vary considerably through things that may, at first glance, not seem that important. They will have a different family position, may be a different gender and may have different school experiences, different teachers and different friendships. They may have seen different things or have been reinforced for certain behaviours. Even experiences that we tend not to think of as being that relevant may well have a significant impact and help to explain the uniqueness of each individual.

THE CONCEPT OF FREE WILL

If you ask most people whether they have free will to make their own choices in life, they would probably answer yes. But do we really have absolutely free choice? We have just considered all the factors that go to make us individual from one another, and many of these will influence the life choices we make.

Answer the following questions.

- Could you be an astronaut?
- Could you be a model?
- Could you own a helicopter?
- Could you be a jockey?
- Could you win the lottery?
- Could you be a brain surgeon?
- Could you travel the world?
- Could you be a university lecturer?
- Could you have your own family?
- Could you live happily ever after?
- Could you do whatever you want, whenever you want?

The answers you will probably give to these questions will be mixed. To some you will answer no, whereas others are possible through a mixture of hard work, luck or opportunity. Among other things, physical appearance, life chances and ability will all determine whether or not we can achieve what we desire and therefore limit the choices available to us.

There are also external constraints that restrict our freedom through laws, rules and regulations. These are *intended* to be for the good of the majority over the minority, although it is worth considering who makes the decision as to what is best for the majority, and whether they are right. This debate has caused countless demonstrations where people have fought to maintain their rights and freedom of choice over the decision makers who, in effect, take away our free will.

Psychologists and philosophers who do not believe that we really have free will suggest our behaviour is determined by the things we have listed above – our genetic inheritance, our biological make-up, our upbringing, and so on. Freud believed that our behaviour was determined by the unconscious forces that are the result of our early childhood, while behaviourists suggest that all our behaviour is shaped by the reinforcers we have received.

The answer probably lies somewhere between the two – some of our behaviours are determined but we still have a certain degree of free will and our ability to think about our life chances actually makes us different from other species. Remember, anyone could own a helicopter if they worked hard enough and anyone could be a jockey, even if they are six feet tall and weigh 16 stone – they would just find it quite difficult to get someone to employ them and they are very unlikely to win any races!

CORE THEORY: humanistic theory

Candidates should be able to:

- distinguish between self-concept and ideal self in relation to self-esteem

- explain the idea of unconditional positive regard

- explain the idea of self-actualisation

- explain the criticisms of humanism as an explanation of the self

- consider trait theory as an alternative theory, with specific reference to extraversion and neuroticism.

HUMANISTIC THEORY

The humanistic approach to psychology developed in the second half of the twentieth century as a response to the Freudian and behaviourist approaches to behaviour.

- You may agree with Freudian theory and feel that you are driven by forces from within.

- You may accept the theory of behaviourism and believe that your life has been shaped by the reinforcement you have received from others.
- You may instead take the humanistic view that, although you have had some constraints on your life opportunities and pressures to behave in certain ways, ultimately you do have the ability to choose how to act – that is, you do have free will.

Humanistic theory focuses on the fact that we, as human beings, are individual and unique, with our own thoughts, feelings and values. Only by understanding how each one of us perceives the world can we understand our personality, our motivations and our behaviours. Trying to explain human beings in any other way misses the essential essence of an individual.

Many personality theories try to categorise people into types and then predict their behaviour. Humanistic theory suggests that we should not do this because we can only categorise people using the tools that are available and these may be inadequate. We like to categorise people by testing them and then scoring their responses in order to give us an easy and simplistic way to make predictions. Humanistic theorists suggest that it may be necessary to use less rigorous techniques in order to investigate the things that really matter to individual human beings.

This approach points out that we are the only people that really know the reasons why we do things, and that for other people to try to interpret our behaviour will often lead them to make mistakes. If you hear someone say to you 'I know why you did that,' they may actually be quite wrong. Humanists believe that we are not only motivated by basic drives such as the need to eat or to protect our property. They also believe that we ultimately strive to be fulfilled and happy.

The humanistic approach also accepts the fact that we do have some constraints on our life choices but, because we were born with free will, we have the ability to make choices.

Imagine you have been raised in an environment where crime is the norm. You may feel pressurised to conform to a criminal way of life by your parents and friends, and you may have seen people rewarded for their criminal activities by having material possessions. You still have the choice as to whether to go along with a criminal way of life because you can actually say 'No, I don't want to.' So you can choose whether to become a model citizen or a criminal, a leader or a follower. It is just that some life choices are easier than others!

The humanistic approach to psychology was developed by Carl Rogers and Abraham Maslow in America during the 1950s. Both were psychologists and Carl Rogers was also a therapist who had been trained as a psychoanalyst (using the principles of Freudian theory).

SELF-CONCEPT, IDEAL SELF AND SELF-ESTEEM

- *Self-concept:* our self-concept is the concept or idea that we have about what and who we are. It begins to develop in early childhood and initially focuses on concrete characteristics such as our physical appearance, our skills and our possessions. As we get older, our self-concept changes as we begin to focus on more abstract attributes such as our confidence, our kindness, how popular we are and our aspirations. It includes an awareness of what we are like and what we can do. This is a central feature of Rogers's theory of personality (see below). Our self-concept is made up not only of factual information but also from our evaluation of ourselves. We might think that we are wonderful and this will have come from comparing ourselves to other people (and also by comparing ourselves with our ideal self – see below). On the other hand, we might feel that we are worthless. Again this will have come from comparisons. This self-concept will have a significant impact on the way we behave because, if we believe we are strong and capable, we are more likely to take on challenges and push ourselves further than if we think we are weak and ineffective. The most important thing to remember about self-concept is that we find it very difficult to see ourselves as others see us and our self-evaluations are not always accurate.
- *Ideal self*: this is how we would like to be – for example, we might want to be tall and good-looking or rich and famous, clever or popular (or all of them).
- *Self-esteem:* our self-esteem comes from comparing our actual self with our ideal self. If your self-concept is positive and you think you are a good and worthwhile human being who is clever and popular, this is quite likely to be close to your ideal self. Therefore your self-esteem will be high. If there is a huge gap between what you think you are like and what you want to be like, your self-esteem will be low.

Unconditional positive regard

What is it that makes some people have high self-esteem, feel good about themselves and feel comfortable in their own skin, whereas others have no self-esteem and very little self-confidence? According to Rogers (1959), parents can have a significant influence on our self-esteem.

If you remember, self-esteem is the difference between who we are and who we would like to be. Rogers suggested that some parents (and also other significant adults) set certain conditions on children by saying things like 'I will only love you if you ...'. This will set the child a target that might be unrealistic – a target that they would ideally like to achieve but perhaps never can. Because the child will have this ideal to strive for, which is totally unrealistic, they are *never* going to be like their ideal self. Therefore the gap between their actual self and their ideal self will be huge and will lead to the child having very low self-esteem.

The way that this can be resolved is for parents to provide unconditional positive regard to the child. By this we mean that there should be no conditions on the parents' love for the child, so they would say 'I love you no matter what you do.' This unconditional love will allow the child to develop their own standards without having these unrealistically forced on them by others.

Self-actualisation

Self-actualisation is the process whereby we strive to reach the utmost pinnacle of success and satisfaction. It is not to do with material possessions, but is more to do with achieving the sense of self-fulfilment and contentment. The majority of us do not manage to achieve self-actualisation because we are too busy striving to survive.

Abraham Maslow's theory

Maslow (1954) talks about self-actualisation, but he suggested that there is a hierarchy of needs that have to be fulfilled before we can gain self-actualisation or self-fulfilment. Figure 5.4 illustrates this

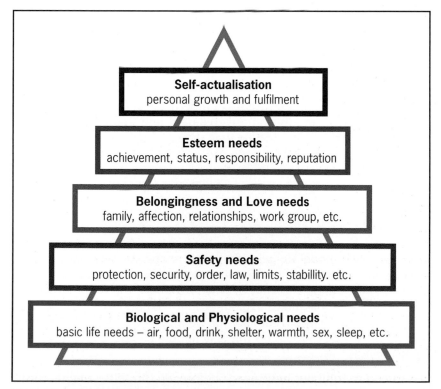

Figure 5.4 Maslow's hierarchy of needs

hierarchy and shows how basic physiological needs such as food and drink come at the bottom of the hierarchy and need to be fulfilled in order for us to climb to the next step of the ladder, which is the need for safety. Towards the top of the hierarchy we get the higher-order needs, such as achievement, status and reputation, and we finally reach the state of self-actualisation when all the other component parts have been satisfied.

According to Maslow, we all strive to reach the stage of self-actualisation where we can fulfil our potential and achieve all we are capable of achieving, but very few people actually reach this state of self-actualisation because we are too busy trying to meet the lower-level needs.

Maslow suggested that we measure self-actualisation by focusing on the number of peak experiences we have. It seems reasonable to suggest that people whose lives are spent simply trying to survive are unlikely to have many of these experiences. By peak experiences, Maslow was referring to those rare occasions when all is right with the world and we feel an inner feeling of pure elation and joy.

CRITICISMS OF HUMANISM AS AN EXPLANATION OF THE SELF

Humanism does not provide an explanation of the causes of our behaviour – for example, we know that self-concept is important, but how does our self-concept affect our actual behaviour? We also know that the humanistic model tends to ignore some of the really important genetic and psychological factors that can affect a person. There is evidence to suggest that we inherit certain characteristics from our parents – predispositions to illness, and so on. We may be motivated to behave in a certain way in order to be accepted by a group, even though we know the group is not held in high regard by the rest of society. We also know that people take drugs as a way to escape from what they consider to be life's difficulties, even though they know that by taking drugs they are likely to shorten their lives and cause themselves pain and suffering – hardly a step towards self-actualisation!

The humanistic model suggests that the only people who can explain their behaviour are the people themselves. However, we do not always have an understanding of why we behave the way that we do. Even when we are asked to explain our motivation using self-reports, these may actually lack credibility (or we may simply lie), so perhaps it is more beneficial to focus on the way people behave and not on what they say.

If we need to fulfil our basic needs before we can self-actualise, this does not explain why artists will go without food in order to continue to paint, or why people will put themselves in positions of extreme danger in order to achieve some sort of extraordinary goal. Michael Reardon, one of the most famous free climbers, who climbed without any sort of ropes or safety gear, found his fulfilment in climbing some of the world's most challenging rock faces. He would be missing out on the lower-level needs such as safety and security in order to put himself at great risk, although perhaps this was his personal 'self-actualisation'.

Finally, if we are dealing with people who have some sort of mental illness, humanists suggest that we would have to spend huge amounts of time with each one, trying to work out what is going on for them and devising an individual plan of treatment to deal with their difficulties. This of course may be an excellent idea, although it will be very time consuming. The client may also find it hard to be honest about how they feel, may have poor language skills and find it hard to express themselves, or they may simply lack insight into their problems. There are people who have traits or difficulties in common and perhaps it is more productive to focus on similarities between groups of people rather than differences in order to support the maximum number of people.

Trait theory

The humanistic belief that we are all individuals suggests that we cannot effectively be grouped together or compared to others because, by doing that, we would lose our uniqueness. However, I am sure that you will have realised that we do share some things in

Figure 5.5 A climber 'free soloing' in White Rock Overlook Park, Los Alamos, New Mexico

It has been documented that pets elicit parental behaviours in children as young as three years of age. A. MacDonald (1981) found that the majority of children in his sample of 31 felt that their dog understood what they were talking about. Ten-year-old children's ability to show empathy could be predicted by the likelihood of these children having intimate talks with a pet.

B.K. Bryant (1982) found that the number of intimate talks children had with their pets could reliably predict their levels of empathy as ten year olds. We cannot be sure that the pet caused the empathy or whether empathetic people choose to own pets.

V.L. Voith (1985) found from a questionnaire study that similar attachment mechanisms occur between people as they do between people and their pets. Reports suggest that pets also seem to miss their owners and were happy upon their return. Owners considered their dogs and cats as family members, and believed everyone in the household was aware of their pets' moods. Even when pets chewed furniture or bit people, their owners kept them, which provided evidence of attachment relationships.

Attachment to pets has also been related to improved health, although this finding was between elderly owners and was not replicated with younger samples.

The authors concluded that the importance of pet owning to child development will not be taken seriously unless methodologically sound research is carried out. Therefore this study aimed to address the problems with previous research on pets by effectively matching groups of preadolescents.

Aim

The aim of this study was to address all the methodological problems of past research by matching pet-owning and non-pet-owning preadolescents on parental marital status, number of siblings and social class, and then to assess self-esteem, self-concept, autonomy and attachment to pets.

Predictions

1. Older participants would score higher than younger participants on measures of autonomy, self-concept and self-esteem (due to normal developmental processes).

2. Increases were expected to be greater for pet owners than for non-pet owners.

3. All participants would indicate a positive regard for pets regardless of whether they owned a pet or not.

4. The pet-owning preadolescents would report greater attachment to pets than non-pet-owning preadolescents.

5. Within the pet-owning group, greater attachment was expected to be related to higher scores on autonomy, self-esteem and self-concept (because greater attachment was suggested to be related to greater well-being).

Method

Background questionnaire

Researchers used an interview and questionnaire to gather background information about the children, such as age, gender and family size, and also pet ownership.

The children were asked to complete a number of psychometric tests, which covered the following:

- autonomy (how independent they were)
- self-concept (the mental picture the children had of themselves, and whether this was positive or negative)
- self-esteem (whether the children had a feeling of self-worth and pride in themselves)
- attachment to animals (how meaningful the relationships were to the children).

Procedure

The authors got permission from the school to perform the study. The participants were given a brief explanation of the purpose of the study, informed of their rights and asked if they would like to volunteer to take part. The ones who agreed were told they could withdraw from the study at any time, although none did.

The children in each class for each grade level were put in groups depending on whether or not they were a pet owner (owning or not owning a cat or dog). They were then put into small groups (two to four subjects) and assigned to an interviewer. They then completed the background questionnaire and the psychometric tests in one session, were debriefed and thanked for participating.

Letters to parents were sent in order to confirm the reported pet status.

Matching

At each grade level pet-owning and non-pet-owning participants were matched on parental marital status, socio-economic status (decided by parents' income and occupation) and number of siblings. The authors explain that matching groups on more than three variables is logistically quite difficult.

From 152 participants, 130 were selected, giving 65 participants in each group. Length of pet ownership for the pet-owning group averaged one year.

Research participants

The children ranged in age from eight to 13 years old and 77.7 per cent were white.

Results

The authors statistically analysed their attempts to match the pet-owning and non-pet-

Number	Third graders	Fourth graders	Fifth graders	Sixth graders
Girls	16	14	12	17
Boys	10	22	22	17
Average age	8 yrs 7 months	9 yrs 6 months	10 yrs 7 months	11 yrs 6 months
Total number	26	36	34	34

Table 5.4 The breakdown of participants into grades

Parental Marital Status	Pet owners	Non-pet owners
Married	55	56
Separated	0	2
Divorced	9	6
Single parent by choice	1	1
Groups were matched by parental marital status. There was no statistically significant difference between the two groups.		

Table 5.5 Descriptive statistics on matching variables by group

owning groups, and concluded that they were not significantly different on parental marital status, socio-economic status and number of siblings.

Prediction 1: The general prediction that older participants would achieve higher scores than younger participants on measures of autonomy, self-concept and self-esteem was partially supported in this study

Autonomy
The results were as follows: pet owners were more likely to perceive their parents as people (*rather than just 'parents'*) than non-pet owners, and the fifth graders were more autonomous (or independent) than the other three grades.

Self-concept
Among the pet-owning groups, the sixth grade had the highest scores for self-concept and their scores were significantly higher than the scores for the non-pet-owning sixth graders. The differences in the other groups were not statistically different.

Self-esteem

For self-esteem, pet owners on average reported higher self-esteem than non-pet owners. The only exception was fourth grade, where the non-pet owners reported higher self-esteem.

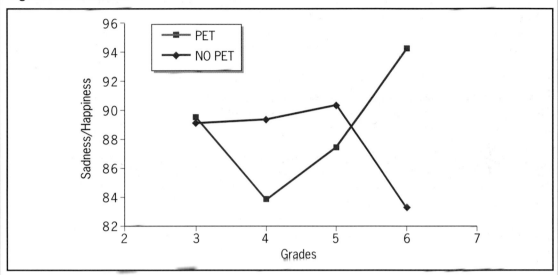

Figure 5.6 The mean scores for measures of self-concept for each school grade (for both pet and non-pet owners)

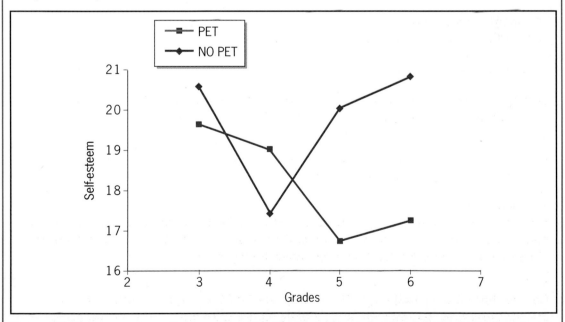

Figure 5.7 The mean scores for measures of self-esteem for each school grade (for both pet and non-pet owners)

Source (Tables 5.4 & 5.5, Figures 5.6 & 5.7): Van Houtte & Jarvis (1995), reproduced with permission

Prediction 2: Increases in scores of autonomy, self-concept and self-esteem were expected to be greater for pet owners than for non-pet owners
The results did not consistently support this prediction, although the sixth-grade pet owners reported higher self-concepts and self-esteem than the non-pet-owning sixth graders.

Prediction 3: All participants were expected to indicate a positive regard for pets regardless of whether they owned a pet or not
The results supported this prediction.

Prediction 4: The pet-owning preadolescents were expected to report greater attachment to pets than non-pet-owning preadolescents
However, the results for attachment to animals (as measured in this study) were not dependent on owning a pet, and suggested that the non-pet owners scored more highly on attachment to pets than the pet owners (see Table 5.6).

	Self-concept Mean	Self-esteem Mean	Attachment Mean
Third			
Pet owner	89.5	19.6	32.7
Non-pet owner	89.1	20.6	33.6
Fourth			
Pet owner	83.8	19.0	28.7
Non-pet owner	89.4	17.5	30.7
Fifth			
Pet owner	87.4	16.7	35.4
Non-pet owner	90.4	20.0	33.9
Sixth			
Pet owner	94.2	17.2	32.8
Non-pet owner	83.2	20.8	32.1
Note Lower mean indicative of greater self-esteem.			

Table 5.6 The results for Predictions 4 and 5

Prediction 5: Within the pet-owning group, greater attachment was expected to be related to higher scores on autonomy, self-esteem and self-concept (because greater attachment was suggested to be related to greater well-being)
No significant correlations were obtained, so there was no support for this prediction.

Table 5.6 gives the results for Predictions 4 and 5. It shows that shows that, among the pet owners, the grade with the highest attachment score (35.4) had lower self-concept but higher self-esteem.

Discussion

The authors focus the first half of the discussion on describing their results. They point out that they successfully matched the groups effectively, which makes this research a significant contribution to the pet literature.

The findings of this study support past research, which suggested that pets generate feelings of being loved and that a pet's behaviour may be viewed by its owner as reinforcing. It may also be viewed as displaying unconditional positive regard (although perhaps if the owners didn't possess a tin opener to get at the Chum, they would love them a little less!). These positive aspects of pet ownership were supported by the results, which showed that pet owners reported higher self-esteem than non-pet owners, and that the pets may have their greatest impact on children's lives as they enter adolescence. The results did not indicate that attachment to animals depended on owning a pet.

The authors found that there was no association between attachment to pets and the perceived positive benefits of owning a pet. They suggest that the presence of a pet, not the degree of attachment pet owners felt, was the important factor.

Implications: suggestions as to the usefulness of the research

Consistent with past research, pet owners reported greater autonomy, so pet ownership may be used to help the development of autonomous characteristics such as responsibility and self-reliance.

Because pets were found to significantly influence self-concept and self-esteem in preadolescents, pets could be used as a source of support in times of stress for individuals with lowered self-concept and self-esteem.

Pets may also be used as substitutes for human support when it is not available.

Further research

The authors make a number of suggestions for further research:

- consideration of ownership of cats and dogs compared to other animals

- studies using wider age ranges of children or undertaking longitudinal studies would provide additional information

- consideration of the effects on self-concept and self-esteem of pet ownership on particular groups of children (e.g. chronically ill children)

- children with special educational needs who go into mainstream classes report a decrease in their self-concept, and research into pet ownership with these children would be useful

- research into pet therapy as an intervention, (for example, with institutionalised older adults who suffer with low autonomy)

- in elderly populations, pets enhance feelings of responsibility; future research could investigate this effect with younger populations.

Limitations of the study

The authors, in their discussion, suggest that their study has the following limitations.

- The authors mention that there are further variables that could confound (*confuse*) the results – for example, the presence of another pet in the household or something about the setting that the families live in that could account for the results. What they meant was that the results may have been caused by something other than animals.

- The study included only cats and dogs, although the non-pet-owning participants may have owned another kind of pet, such as gerbils or rabbits, which may have influenced their reports of their relations to pets. The questionnaire did not ask them about other pets.

- The technique used by the authors to measure attachment to pets consisted of only six items that had been used with elderly participants who were required to give yes/no answers. This study used the same measure although the authors changed the responses to a seven-point Likert scale. Was the technique satisfactory for children?

- This research was intended to look at measures of various parts of our personality and whether they are affected by pet ownership. This involved measuring one person's personality and comparing to someone else's personality. This suggests that we are comparable, and you may think that we can't be compared and are actually totally unique.

- The authors did not specify who completed the questionnaires although it would seem likely that it was the children themselves. Perhaps the children were not honest in their answers, or perhaps they responded with what they thought the researchers wanted to hear.

- The total number of pupils that took part was only 130, and they were divided into eight groups (four grades and pet owners/non-pet owners). Therefore each group was quite small and the age groups were very young. Although the authors said they carefully matched the groups, there may have been other factors that had not been taken into consideration.

Generally the results supported the predictions, but some of the results actually contradicted what the researchers had predicted. For example, the non-pet owners in grade four had higher self-esteem than the pet owners. The researchers could not explain these results.

APPLICATION OF RESEARCH INTO THE SELF: COUNSELLING

Candidates should be able to:
- explain how psychological research relates to counselling, e.g. raising self-esteem in depressed people, individual choice in careers counselling, humanistic principles of relationship counselling.

WHAT IS COUNSELLING?

Counselling is a process whereby a client and a counsellor, through talking, explore a difficulty the client may be having that affects their life. Counselling does not involve one person advising the other what to do or directing them in any way. For counselling to be effective, the counsellor acts as a kind of facilitator to help the client explore their situation, perhaps looking at it in a different way, and to reach their own conclusions as to the best way to deal with their problems. The reason for this is because, as a species, unless we have to, we are unlikely to do anything we really don't want to do.

The sessions take place in a private and confidential setting, and have to be at the request of the client. The counsellor will listen carefully, clarifying what the client is saying if necessary. They do not judge the client. Many of the emotions that the client feels can be expressed in a counselling setting, whereas they may not be able to express them in other settings without things becoming difficult for the client. This involves a great degree of trust between client and counsellor.

The terms counselling and therapy are often used interchangeably. Counselling tends to be a shorter course of sessions, often exploring more specific difficulties and taking a more focused approach. On the other hand, therapy (short for psychotherapy) tends to be more long term and much more in depth, helping the client gain insight into their problems.

Counsellors learn about different theoretic perspectives and some may favour the theory of Freud, whereas others may believe in behaviourism as an explanation of behaviour. Depending on which perspective the counsellor favours, this will influence the way they perceive the client's difficulties.

Depression

We say we are suffering from depression when we feel 'low' or miserable, tearful or even hopeless. However, we all feel depressed at some time in our lives, although it is usually in response to some experience or event such as the death of someone important to us or the end of a significant relationship. When the feeling of depression is out of proportion to the event, or if it continues for a prolonged period of time, the causes may be more complex. In fact considerable research evidence has indicated that people with low self-esteem are very likely to suffer from depression.

The psychiatrist Aaron Beck (1967) believes that depression is caused by the way people feel about themselves and their world. If they feel that they are worthless and they believe that things are not going to get better, this will affect their attitude to the whole of their life. If you remember, the way we evaluate our self-worth comes from comparing our actual self with our ideal self. If we feel that we are worthless and very different to our ideal self, we will have low self-esteem.

We also mentioned that our self-evaluations are not always accurate. These evaluations may come from the expectations of other people. If you remember, people who believe that they will only get unconditional positive regard from significant others if they do as

Figure 5.8 A counsellor at work

others want them to do, may end up with distorted ways of thinking about themselves. They may also have too high expectations of themselves, which they find they cannot live up to, and so their ideal self will be very different from their actual self.

One way to help people who are suffering with low self-esteem is to assist them in re-evaluating their worth and support them in thinking about themselves differently. The main reason for this is because the way we think influences the way we behave.

Earlier in this chapter (page 220) we talked about cognitive behavioural therapy (CBT) as a means of treating phobias. If you remember, this kind of therapy aims to change what we think (cognitions), which will ultimately change how we act (behaviours). CBT was first proposed by Beck in the 1960s and is now considered one of the most effective forms of treatment, not only for phobias, but for many of the emotional and mental health problems of today, including depression. The following is an example of how CBT could work, by helping a depressed client challenge their negative automatic way of thinking.

Imagine that you think you are worthless, and people can't be bothered with you and don't want to be with you (you have a poor self-concept and low self-esteem), you are likely to feel really sad and depressed, which in turn will make you behave in a way that is less sociable. Your behaviour will appear to others to be aloof and unfriendly, which will make them believe that you are standoffish and antisocial, which, in turn, makes people less willing to interact with you, which will reinforce your thoughts that you are worthless … and so on (see Figure 5.9).

Table 5.7 shows how the aim of CBT would be to help the client think about the situation in a different way.

By thinking differently, the client in Table 5.7 has behaved differently, which has caused them to feel very differently about the situation. If

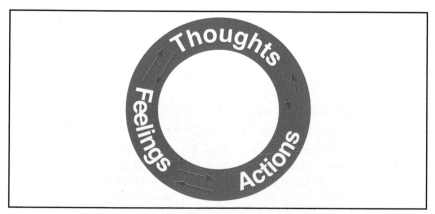

Figure 5.9 The cycle of how thoughts, feelings and actions relate to each other

Situation	You are walking down the corridor at school/work and someone you know totally ignores you	
	Normal depressed thoughts (unhelpful)	**New way of thinking (helpful)**
Thoughts	They ignored me because I am not worth talking to and they can't be bothered with me	Perhaps the person has had some bad news and they were too preoccupied to notice me
Emotional feelings	Miserable and rejected	Concerned
Physical	Sick feeling in the stomach	No physical symptoms – feel fine
Action	Try to avoid them in the future	Try to contact the person to make sure they are OK

Table 5.7 How CBT helps the client think about a sample situation in a different way

the person they contact then responds in a positive way to their concern, this will enhance their self-esteem.

Interestingly, the results of the core study in this section also have implications for raising self-esteem. Van Houtte and Jarvis found that their child participants' self-reports showed that those who owned pets had higher self-esteem. This may be because the children's pets generate feelings of being loved and display unconditional positive regard. The significant differences between the different age groups suggested that pets may have their greatest impact on children's lives as they enter adolescence.

Individual choice in careers counselling

Careers counsellors are qualified professionals who help individuals to choose the right career for them. They will ask questions about skills, interests, life plans and motivation. They may also use some personality tests to identify the traits of their clients. From the responses they get, they support their clients to make positive career choices.

From the information we have covered so far in this chapter, you will probably realise that careers counselling must be based on the needs of each individual rather than a group. Although we know we do have things in common, the unique mixture of traits we have will make us all different from each other, and the careers counsellor will have the skills to identify the most appropriate direction for their clients. A counsellor will also ensure that their clients set realistic targets for themselves rather than be persuaded to take a certain path by others. If someone is pressurised into following a certain course, they will be less motivated and therefore less likely to succeed, which will, in turn, impact on their self-esteem.

There are however, some careers that suit some people more than others. If we take the extraversion/introversion trait, for example, research evidence has shown that introverts are better at tasks that require prolonged periods of concentration (such as air traffic controllers). On the other hand, people who wish to work in sales need to be extravert and outgoing.

Humanistic principles of relationship counselling

Psychological research has impacted not only on individual counselling but also on relationship counselling, as many of the difficulties we experience are a direct result of poor relationships. Human beings, being inherently social creatures, often become very distressed when their relationships are unsatisfactory.

Humanistic principles focus on the fact that each individual's natural tendency is to aim for self-actualisation. Therefore the difficulties in a relationship might be caused by one person blocking the potential of the other, which in turn will set up tensions between the two. The humanistic counsellor will help the clients to see the situation and come to their own solutions as they are best placed to find the answers. The aim will be to help the clients have an awareness of their underlying emotions and motives without interpreting or judging their behaviours, and to allow them to achieve self-actualisation.

Humanistic counsellors are also known as client-centred therapists for the reason that their focus is on the client. Carl Rogers suggested that they need to have empathy (being able to put themselves in the position of the other person and see things from their point of view), warmth and genuineness.

Research in psychology

Hugh Coolican (1996) says there are three major ways in which psychologists obtain information about people: 'You ask them, watch them or meddle.' This chapter describes the methods used by psychologists when they watch *and* meddle.

Because psychology is a science, and therefore uses the scientific method, psychologists working with both people and animals need to remember that neither of them are predictable, unlike chemicals or inanimate objects, and so the techniques that psychologists use have to be well designed and carefully conducted.

- The first section in this chapter looks at different types of research, some of which make it easy to keep a high degree of control and others that are devised to study how people behave naturally. We will also need to be aware that some pieces of research generate information that is easy to count (or quantify), whereas others focus more on experience. We will need to decide how to choose the most appropriate method for research.
- The second section is written to help you to plan and carry out your own research, by discussing different methodologies and the analysis of results. It also identifies what you will need to know for the OCR GCSE examination, as you will need to be able to plan and carry out an experiment, plan, administer and collect data from a questionnaire, carry out an interview and carry out an observation.

UNIT B543

RESEARCH METHODS USED IN PSYCHOLOGY

OVERVIEW

As part of the OCR examination, you will need to have a good understanding of the techniques chosen by psychologists, and to be aware of the strengths and weaknesses of each technique. We will begin by looking at different types of research, some of which make it easy to keep a high degree of control, while others are devised to study how people behave naturally.

You will also need to be aware that some pieces of research generate information which is easy to count (or quantify), whereas others focus more on experience. You will need to decide how to choose the most appropriate method for research.

KEY CONCEPTS

The OCR examination requires candidates to be able to:

- distinguish between independent variables and dependent variables
- outline what is meant by an extraneous variable
- explain how extraneous variables can be controlled, including standardisation.

RESEARCH TECHNIQUES

Experiments

The first technique we should consider is how to conduct an experiment – a technique whereby psychologists can actually start to meddle! The experiment has been widely used in psychology because the psychologist has greater control over what happens, and can therefore test cause and effect and so make some intelligent guesses about *why* things happen and *why* people behave in the way they do. Experiments are usually chosen to investigate topics such as memory and perception.

In order to explain how experiments work, it might be useful to think of something we could investigate and then consider how best to conduct our research. Let's consider the suggestion that we find it harder to learn things, retain and remember them (encode, store and retrieve them, see Chapter 2, page 42) when we are very tired. I think most of us might be familiar with this suggestion!

Independent variable (IV) and dependent variable (DV)

When planning any experiment (in psychology, biology, chemistry or physics) the researcher will alter one variable (called the **independent variable**) and then measure what effect this has on another variable (called the **dependent variable**).

In our experiment, we want to look at the effects of sleep on memory. We need to think how we are going to test participants' memory and, also, how we are going to manipulate their tiredness. We could test memory by seeing how many words people will remember. We could also manipulate tiredness by giving some people a good night's sleep while others have to stay up or are woken after a couple of hours.

- In this instance the independent variable (the thing we are manipulating) is the amount of sleep people get.
- The dependent variable depends on what the researcher manipulates, and it is what the researcher measures. The way we could test people's memory is by looking at the number of words they remember from a list, therefore their scores would be the dependent variable.

In any research, it is important to carefully consider the manipulation of the independent variable and also how to measure the dependent variable. These measures might be, for example, the time spent looking at something, the number of words recalled, the time taken to complete a task, the number of positive reinforcements or the level of shock given.

Measuring behaviour is more complex – for example, measuring aggression. The psychologist needs to define what behaviours are to be considered aggressive – for example, physical aggression (pushing, kicking, hitting) and verbal aggression (shouting and swearing – although the first may not actually be aggressive, it may be in excitement or trying to attract someone's attention). Once the behaviour is effectively defined, how will it be measured: in terms of how often it occurs or how long it lasts, or both?

It is worth noting that if you have used a non-experimental design, such as a **naturalistic observation** or a **correlational study**, there is no independent variable, but you will still have an expectation which you are testing.

Extraneous variables

Extraneous variables, or extra variables, are variables that are likely to affect the results of the investigation because they have not been controlled by the researchers. They are also known as confounding variables, because they can confound (or confuse) the results.

Let's look in more depth at what we mean by extraneous variables. To be confident that the IV has actually caused the DV, the researcher must control all other aspects of the experiment because, if they don't, they cannot be sure that the results are really **valid**. For example, in a study of memory, we find that one condition has much higher scores than the other. When we look more closely at the two groups of participants, we may find that one group of participants is actually much older than the other group. These age differences, which were not controlled for, will affect the results.

Some of the other variables researchers need to consider are listed below.

- **Situational variables:** sometimes aspects of the environment may affect the participants' performance, for example if it is too hot, too cold, too familiar or very unfamiliar and therefore frightening.
- **Participant variables:** if groups of participants vary significantly, this could affect the results. For example, if one group of participants with poor eyesight were asked to do a task involving visual discrimination, this could affect their performance and the results. Researchers have different techniques to make sure that this does not happen, and these are described in the section on experimental design (page 252).
- **Standardised procedure:** each participant must be treated in exactly the same way, each doing exactly the same tasks, with the same materials, in exactly the same order. This reduces the variables in the procedure.
- **Standardised instructions:** every participant must be given exactly the same instructions, ideally by the same person and in the same way. One way of ensuring standardisation is to provide written instructions, which should be simple and clear.

KEY CONCEPTS

The OCR examination requires candidates to be able to:

- describe the use of laboratory experiments
- describe the use of field experiments
- describe the strengths and weaknesses of laboratory and field experiments.

Types of experiment

We have just looked at how to measure and control variables but, in reality, psychologists never have full control of all the variables. This becomes apparent as we examine the different types of experiment described below.

Laboratory experiment

In the laboratory experiment there is a high level of control of variables in order to gain the most valid results possible. The psychologist manipulates the IV (the independent variable), decides where the experiment will take place, at what time and with which participants, in what circumstances, and using a standardised procedure. This standardisation may create **demand characteristics**. These are features of the research that may affect participants' behaviour, so they may act unnaturally or look for cues to tell them what the research is about and behave accordingly.

Field experiment

In a field experiment the psychologist manipulates the IV but the experiment takes place in a real-life setting, so there is less control over variables such as the people who take part, unexpected environmental changes and so on.

You will see below that what is a disadvantage in one type of experiment becomes an advantage in another.

Strengths

In a laboratory experiment it is much easier to control all aspects of the experiment and counteract any extraneous or confounding variables.

In field experiments researchers can see how people behave naturally as a result of any manipulation.

Weaknesses

Because laboratory experiments are artificial, this may affect participants' behaviour and produce results that do not apply to real life. For example, if participants know they are taking part in an experiment they may be affected by demand characteristics. People, particularly children, do not always follow instructions exactly, which may well affect the results. Therefore researchers have to be very cautious in interpreting their results and applying them in real situations.

Also, in field experiments the researcher cannot be sure that the results are due to their manipulation because there are so many other uncontrolled variables.

KEY CONCEPTS

The OCR examination requires candidates to be able to:

- describe the use of questionnaires as a method of self-report
- distinguish between open and closed questions
- describe the strengths and weaknesses of questionnaires.

Experimental design

In any sort of scientific experiment, the data (results) are compared from two (or sometimes more) sources. In psychological research, data are gathered from the participants who are taking part. Sometimes, one group of participants experiences the IV (called the **experimental condition**) and the other group does not (this is the **control condition**). For example, in our research into the effects of tiredness on memory, one group of participants would have had a normal night's sleep while the other group would have been sleep deprived.

The way in which participants are assigned to groups is called the **experimental design**. The three types of experimental design are described below.

Sometimes we use this design when the people naturally fall into two different groups, such as males and females, Nottingham Forest supporters and Arsenal supporters. In this case we cannot allocate people to one condition or the other we can still use the design and the statistical tests that go with it.

Independent-groups design

Independent-groups or independent-measures design is the name for the design where there are different participants in each group. In **laboratory** and some field experiments the researcher will manipulate the IV and choose which participants are assigned to the experimental group and which to the control group. This should be done by **random allocation**, which ensures that each participant has an equal chance of being assigned to one group or the other (for details of randomising, see the section on sampling below, page 269).

When participants are assigned randomly to their group, one group may contain more alert or skilled participants. We know that these **participant variables** might be responsible for differences between the results from the two groups that are not related to the IV. Therefore a large **sample** is needed to reduce this effect.

If there is a variable that may directly affect the results (such as eyesight) then a pre-test should be done to ensure that the variable is equally distributed between the two conditions.

Strengths

The independent measures design is the quickest and easiest way of allocating participants to groups; there are no order effects (which occur with repeated measures, see below).

Weaknesses

Participant variables may affect the results, but using a large sample to counteract this makes the research more expensive and time consuming, as does a pre-test.

Repeated-measures design

Here every participant goes through the experimental and the control conditions. This is an advantage because as the same people are in both conditions there are no participant variables and no need for pre-testing. However, there is a drawback: participants may behave differently after they experience one condition and thus affect the results – this is called **order effects** or **practice effects**.

To get around this problem the researcher counterbalances the order of the conditions for the participants. The sample is split into two: one half does the experimental condition (A), then the control condition (B); the other half does the control condition (B), then the experimental condition (A). This is called the ABBA design – it cancels out any order effects.

Strengths

Repeated-measures design eliminates the effect of participant variables; it is therefore possible to have a fairly small sample.

Weaknesses

Because of order effects, counterbalancing must be employed; participants may decide not to return for the second part of the experiment; this design cannot be used in quasi or natural experiments because participants automatically fall into one of two conditions.

Matched-pairs design

One way to get over the difficulties of the above designs is to use a technique called the matched-pairs design. This uses different participants in each group but they are matched in pairs on the basis of variables relevant to the study, such as age, gender, intelligence, reading ability or socio-economic background. One of each pair is then assigned to the experimental condition and the other to the control condition. The perfect matched-pairs design is one that uses identical (monozygotic, or MZ) twins. To find out more about twin studies turn to Chapter 1, page 24.

Strengths

A fairly small sample will be enough, though more participants may be needed to go through the pre-tests in order to find good matches; the effects of individual differences are reduced; there are no order effects.

Weaknesses

It can be expensive and time consuming; accurate matching is quite difficult and participant variables may still affect results.

Questionnaires

Questionnaires are used as a form of **self-report** when **respondents** (the people answering the questions) provide information about themselves without necessarily having to talk to another person. Questionnaires can be used to gather information from individuals or groups, and may be used as part of a study. The questionnaire, once written, will be given to a representative sample of the population in order to find out what the 'average' answers would be. The answers given by the respondents can then be compared to the average to see if they are in some way different or unusual.

The questions must be carefully prepared so that they are clear and do not persuade the respondents to answer in a particular way. The researcher might first do a pilot study with the questions, giving them to a few people and asking for comments. She or he can then adjust them for the main study if necessary.

In order to reduce **demand characteristics** (see page 280), which might encourage respondents to give the answers they think the researcher wants, the questionnaire may be given a general title such as 'A study of children's toys' when the survey is actually trying to find out whether parents encourage their children to play with toys related to their gender. In addition, a few questions may be included that check for the honesty of the respondent by asking the same question in a different way.

Types of question

The questions may be closed or open-ended, depending on the kind of information the researcher wants.

- **Closed questions** produce clear-cut answers that are easy to interpret and quantify, such as 'Is your child happy at school? – yes/no.' Respondents may want to answer 'Well, it depends,' yet because they are forced to choose yes or no, their answer will not reflect their real opinions. A compromise is the question that provides a range of answers, perhaps using a scale from 1–5 to reflect the strength or amount of agreement. This provides more detailed information, which is still easy to quantify.

(a) Please tick the box that applies to you				
	Not at all	A little	Quite a lot	Very much
Do you enjoy sports?				
Do you enjoy watching TV?				
Do you enjoy walking?				

(b) Please tick the box that applies to you where 1 = not at all and 5 = very much					
	1	2	3	4	5
Do you enjoy sports?					
Do you enjoy watching TV?					
Do you enjoy walking?					

Table 6.1 These questions use (a) a range of answers and (b) a scale; (a) forces participants to choose one way or the other, whereas (b) allows them to remain indifferent

- **Open-ended questions** give the respondent the opportunity to provide a lot of information and are useful for in-depth research – for example, 'What do you think of your child's school?' However, it would be difficult to compare with other people's answers, so the open-ended question is less useful when trying to quantify information.

Strengths

Questionnaires are quick and easy to operate; a very large sample can be used and they are useful for gathering data quickly and easily; people who are geographically distant can be studied; questionnaires can open up new ideas for further research.

Weaknesses

The sample may be biased because it relies on people returning the questionnaires (they may be returned by people who have plenty of time or strong feelings about the topic); people may not give honest or accurate answers; people may not understand the questions correctly; and some may not return the questionnaires at all.

KEY CONCEPTS

The OCR examination requires candidates to be able to:

- describe the use of interviews as a method of self-report
- distinguish between structured and unstructured interviews
- describe the strengths and weaknesses of interviews.

Interviews

In an interview, the researcher asks the questions face to face and the structure of the interview can vary.

Types of interview

- Structured interviews consist of a series of fixed questions with a limited range of possible answers, much like a questionnaire. They are the fastest to complete and, if well prepared, provide data that are easy to quantify and analyse; but they suffer from the drawbacks of closed questions.
- Unstructured interviews are more like spontaneous conversations. The researcher knows what topics they wish to cover, but they do not have to ask the questions or cover the topics in any order. They can adjust the interview according to the type of responses provided by the participant and can rephrase questions if necessary. They are also able to ask follow-up questions or clarify answers that are ambiguous or contradictory. This technique was used by Piaget in his work with children (see Chapter 3, page 113).

Strengths

In unstructured interviews the interviewer can clarify questions and ambiguous answers, and obtain a wealth of information that the participant might not have provided in a pencil-and-paper exercise.

Weaknesses

Although this technique provides detailed information, its results should not be generalised to the population as a whole, and it is possible that the interviewer may bias the response or misinterpret the answers that are given. The respondents may give the answers they think the interviewer wants **(socially desirable answers)** rather than truthful answers. This method is also time consuming and expensive.

KEY CONCEPTS

The OCR examination requires candidates to be able to:

- describe the use of observations
- identify the differences between covert and overt observations, and between participant and non-participant observations
- describe the strengths and weaknesses of different types of observations.

Observations

When psychologists want to try to understand the way people behave in certain situations they may choose to watch their participants and analyse their behaviour. In fact, sometimes observation can be used as the starting point for an enquiry. It is essential that observers are objective and that their observations are accurate. It is usual to have more than one observer because behaviour is complex, and the observer may be biased or may even miss some of the behaviours while recording what they have seen. If the behaviour is video-taped, the observers will analyse the behaviour from the video. They need to be trained in how to analyse and measure the behaviour being studied so that they all interpret it in the same way. This is called **inter-rater reliability**.

The researchers must decide what behaviours are to be noted (see the section on measuring the dependent variable, Chapter 6, page 249), how the participants will be observed and over what time period. Is it better to watch six children for a 15-minute period or two children for a full playgroup session, or any child who comes to the sandpit? Researchers may choose to run a **pilot study** because they can watch the kind of behaviour they will be analysing, and thus devise an **observation schedule** in order to categorise and measuring that behaviour.

Table 6.2 shows a simple schedule for observing nursery children playing, in order to see which toys were favoured by each child; each participant is identified by a number in order to preserve anonymity (see the section on ethical issues on page 263).

Participant Number	Number of times behaviour observed in a 30-minute period					
	Played with cars	Played with dolls	Looked at books	Played with bricks	Played in the home corner	Played in the sandpit
1 Boy						
2 Boy						
3 Boy						
4 Girl						
5 Girl						
6 Girl						

Table 6.2 Example of a simple schedule

The observational method can be used for a variety of purposes, as described below.

Overt and covert observations

If the participants know that they are being observed, this would be known as an **overt observation**. If the participants are not aware that they are being observed, perhaps because the researchers are hiding, this is called a **covert observation**.

Strengths

Participants behave more naturally if they are in their normal environment, especially if they are not aware they are being watched.

Weaknesses

Participants often know they are being watched and they may behave differently to normal. This is known as being subjected to **observer effects**.

Participant observations

Here the observer becomes one of the group, interacting with the people that he or she wishes to observe.

Strengths

In participant research, the researcher gets a better insight into what is going on because he or she is interacting with the participants all the time.

Weaknesses

In participant research, the researcher may not be objective as she or he will understand more about the behaviour and therefore may interpret it differently. Also in participant research, the presence of the observer may affect the behaviour of the subjects, especially if the observer interacts with them.

Naturalistic observation

Here the researchers have no control – they are not participants but look at behaviour that occurs naturally, as it would in a school playground for example. Before starting the study, the observers try to become familiar to those they are observing, in order to minimise the effect that their presence may have on the behaviour of the participants.

Strengths

The behaviour occurs in its natural setting; observation provides very detailed information; it can be used as a starting point for further, more controlled, research; it can be used when other methods might be unethical.

Weaknesses

The presence of observers could influence the behaviour of those being observed; it is difficult for observers to be completely objective;

many variables could affect behaviour so that it is not possible to draw any conclusions.

KEY CONCEPTS

The OCR examination requires candidates to be able to:

* describe the use of case studies
* describe the use of correlation studies.
* compare the use of longitudinal studies and cross-sectional studies.

Case studies

The case study is an in-depth study of one person or a small number of people. It may include observations or interviews (using open-ended questions) of the person being studied, as well as others who can provide information about the person's past or present experiences and behaviours. Data provided by school or medical records may also be gathered.

Case studies are often used for investigating people who show unusual abilities or difficulties. The second core study in Chapter 3, by Watson and Rayner (1920), considered the 'creation' of a phobia in one small boy.

Strengths

It gives a detailed picture of the individual; by studying those who are unusual, psychologists can discover more about what is usual; it helps in discovering how a person's past may be related to the present; it can be useful in treating individual problems; it can form the basis for future research.

Weaknesses

It often relies on retrospective evidence, which is evidence that has to be remembered and therefore may be of poor quality or distorted; the information gained about one person cannot be generalised to apply to other people; it relies on participants telling the truth; the interviewer may be biased if he or she is looking for certain information.

Correlational study

Psychologists sometimes want to find out what behaviours go together – for example, to see whether the amount of violent television watched is related to the amount of aggression shown. The psychologist must find an accurate way of measuring both variables and then calculate a correlation (relationship) between the two. In our example, data would be gathered by asking participants about their viewing habits, or monitoring their television watching and then either observing their aggressive behaviour or asking others to rate it.

Patterns of correlation

There are two patterns of correlation:

1. a positive correlation occurs when one variable increases as the other increases
2. a negative correlation occurs when one variable increases as the other decreases.

The relationship can be plotted on a scattergram (see Figure 6.6, for examples). If there is no upward or downward pattern in the scores, the indication is that the two variables are not related – this is called a zero correlation. It is important to remember that a correlational study can only show a relationship between two variables; we cannot assume that one variable *causes* the other. However, if there is a high correlation we can use one variable to predict the value of another.

Longitudinal study

A longitudinal study enables researchers to study the same individuals over a period of time, which can be from months to years.

What are longitudinal studies used for?

It is a technique often used for case studies, studies of small groups or studies of **cohorts** (people with a common characteristic, such as a class of pupils).

Strengths

A longitudinal study can allow us to see the long-term effects of an experience; it allows us to learn about developmental changes; characteristics that persist and those that tend to disappear can be identified; there are no participant variables to cause concern as the same people are looked at over time; people can be studied in considerable depth.

Weaknesses

Some participants will drop out over the years, so their data will be of limited use; long-term funding is necessary and may be hard to find; it is difficult to change the study once it is under way; findings may be out of date by the time the study is finished; changes in the participants' lifestyle (e.g. marriage), may affect the variables being measured.

Cross-sectional study

A cross-sectional study also investigates change over time, but does so by comparing people who are at different ages or stages, and studying them all together.

An example of a cross-sectional study

For example, to study changes that occur as children grow up, four-, eight-, 12- and 16-year-olds can be studied at the same time. In contrast, a longitudinal study would take 12 years to complete.

Strengths

Cross-sectional studies provide immediate results; they are cheaper than longitudinal studies; there is less likelihood of participants dropping out; there are less likely to be major changes in the lives of participants that would affect results.

Weaknesses

There are individual differences between groups, which can bias results (although a large sample will reduce this); social changes may create differences between groups (the seven-year olds may have experienced major educational change that the 12-year-olds have not); it tends to exaggerate differences between ages.

SUMMARY

In this part of the chapter we have described some of the main methods that psychologists use to collect data. None of these methods will give us perfect data and be able to give us clear answers to our questions about behaviour. Don't be put off by this because when you think about it, people do things for all manner of reasons and we can't hope to have simple answers to the complex questions about *why* a person behaves in the way they do. Although none of the methods is perfect, they all give us some useful evidence about people and their behaviours. It is our job to make the best sense of that and try to understand a little more about ourselves and others.

PLANNING, PRESENTING AND EVALUATING RESEARCH

UNIT **B543**

OVERVIEW

In the first part of this chapter, we considered the techniques used by psychologists when investigating the human brain and human behaviour. We considered different methodologies, and looked at the strengths and weaknesses of these approaches.

This part of the chapter is written to help you to plan and carry out your own research, by discussing different methodologies and the analysis of results. It also identifies what you will need to know for the OCR GCSE examination, as you will need to be able to plan and carry out an experiment, plan, administer and collect data from a questionnaire, carry out an interview and carry out an observation.

PLANNING RESEARCH

When psychologists want to find out more about a topic they first read the work of other psychologists. They may find that nobody has studied exactly what interests them, or that someone has, but there were flaws in the study that affected the results. They would then plan their own research, recording what they do and what they find, then write it up as a report. This may be published in a psychology journal so that other psychologists can read it and benefit from it, and this is how psychological knowledge is spread and developed.

As you will have seen in the core studies, psychologists who plan and conduct their own investigations will provide an introduction describing the theory and research upon which their work is based. This puts the current research in context and also allows the psychologists to evaluate their findings against previous studies. You will not need to write an introduction yourself, but it is important to consider the work of others when planning your own research.

You will also need to answer questions about a piece of research that will be described in the examination.

We are going to start with information on the ethical considerations, because whenever you plan investigations, you must be mindful of the welfare of your participants.

KEY CONCEPTS

The OCR examination requires candidates to be able to:

- discuss the issues of informed consent and right to withdraw
- discuss the Issues of confidentiality
- discuss the issues of protection of participants, including deception, and health and well-being.

ETHICAL ISSUES

Ethics are judgements about what is right or wrong, good or bad, acceptable or unacceptable. One important area where ethics are discussed is how professional workers such as medical staff, teachers or psychologists, for example, carry out their work. Another area where ethics are important is when we carry out research. To behave ethically when conducting research, we must treat others with respect and concern for their well-being; we must not take advantage of their trust or their lack of knowledge. Unethical behaviour discredits psychology and the work of other psychologists. People may refuse to help with future research if they have been offended by unethical experiments. Ethical concerns apply to both humans and animals, though our focus here is on humans.

Ethical guidelines have been drawn up by the British Psychological Society (BPS) and the Association for the Teaching of Psychology (ATP). All people carrying out psychological research, whether they are a professor of psychology or a student new to the subject, must take account of ethical guidelines. These are summarised below under the 'four Cs': competence, consent, confidentiality and conduct.

Competence

Psychologists and psychology students must work within their limits and be very cautious about giving advice, as people tend to think that anyone studying psychology is able to advise them on their problems. It is one of the hazards of studying psychology that people believe that you are learning how to read minds and deal with their personal problems. You can do neither of these things – and most psychologists can't do them either.

Consent and deception

Participants should be volunteers; they should be informed as to what the research is about and what they will be asked to do before they are asked to consent to take part – this is called **informed consent**. People should not be **deceived** into taking part by being told the study is about something else, or by ignoring aspects of the study that might affect their willingness to take part. Sometimes it is necessary to withhold information from the participant or they will guess what the research is about and therefore behave differently to normal. If this is necessary, before the research is carried out, it should be discussed with people who would be suitable participants (but who haven't been selected) to see if they feel that the research is fair and that the eventual participants are not going to be harmed in any way.

After the research, participants should be **debriefed** so they know what the study was about; their own results should be available to them and the researcher must answer any questions they may have.

Some people, such as children or those with special needs, may be unable to give informed consent. They must be asked if they are willing to help you, but full consent must be gained from whoever is responsible for that person, such as a parent or carer.

Research that is to be carried out in an institution such as a school, factory or supermarket must also be approved by the responsible authority in the institution.

Observations form part of psychological research and consent is not necessary when **observing** people in public, as they could be observed by anyone. However, it is better to get consent to observe if this can be obtained without affecting the behaviour of the participants and therefore ruining the study.

Participants should be told they have the **right to withdraw** from a research study at any time, and be reminded of this right during a long study, especially if they appear to be distressed or uncomfortable. The researcher should stop the study if participants are uncomfortable or distressed, even if they have not asked to withdraw.

Debriefing

After the research, participants should be debriefed so that they know what the study was about; their own results should be available to them and the researcher must answer any questions they have.

Confidentiality

Information about the identity of the participants and any data gained from them must remain confidential. It is unethical to give information about a participant to someone else (such as another researcher) without that person's consent. Data should not be accessible to others and participants should be identified by a number or letter in the research report, in order to protect their anonymity.

Conduct

Participants must be protected, so researchers must ensure that any equipment is safe to use, and that participants are not asked to do anything that is illegal or might affect their health or wellbeing. Nor should participants experience psychological harm, such as distress, fear, anger, embarrassment or offence. Great care should be taken with children, as they are particularly vulnerable and may be unhappy or harmed by experiences that adults would find problem-free.

All participants should leave the investigation feeling as good about themselves as when they started it.

Researchers should be honest about their abilities and competence. They must never make up their own data or use someone else's data and claim it is their own.

KEY CONCEPTS

The OCR examination requires candidates to be able to:

- state the hypothesis for an investigation
- describe and justify the sample used in an investigation
- describe ethical issues involved in an investigation
- describe and justify how the variables are measured in an investigation
- describe and justify the control of extraneous variables in an investigation
- describe the procedure used in an investigation
- explain the strengths and weaknesses of the method used in an investigation
- describe how data are analysed in an investigation.

DESIGNING YOUR OWN RESEARCH

Now you have an understanding of the ethical considerations necessary to protect your participants, you are ready to design your own research. The previous section gave you an overview of different techniques used by psychologists, but there are lots of details that need to be addressed when planning research; we are now going to consider these and look at the information that needs to be included when writing up a piece of research. It is important to remember that all research must be replicable – that is, it can be repeated in order to check the validity of the results and to make sure that the same results that would be obtained if the research should happen to be repeated. In order to be able to replicate the research, every detail has to be accurately recorded.

There are a number of ways of writing a research report, but information is usually provided under the following headings in this order:

- Title
- Introduction (including Hypothesis or Research Aims)
- Method (including Design, Participants, Materials and Procedure)
- Results
- Discussion
- Appendix
- References or Bibliography.

In order to give an example of how to plan a piece of research, it might be helpful to consider the following example.

Idea: when we provide people with organised information, it might be the case that they are more likely to remember it than if they are given the same information in a disorganised format. To give an example, below is an organised list of words and underneath it is the same list but with no organisation.

Animals	Clothes	Colours	Furniture
Cow	Jeans	Pink	Stool
Pig	Socks	Green	Wardrobe
Bear	Skirt	Blue	Table
Horse	Sweatshirt	Yellow	Bed

Blue	Horse	Pink	Table
Cow	Skirt	Stool	Jeans
Socks	Wardrobe	Pig	Clothes
Furniture	Bear	Colours	Bed
Green	Sweatshirt	Yellow	Animals

Which list do you think would be easier to remember?

Independent and dependent variables

In the previous section, on page 249, you read about independent and dependent variables. You will need to remember this information because the first consideration in this type of research is to identify your variables.

In this example, you will need to give some participants the organised list and some the randomly arranged list: therefore, the 'thing' you are manipulating is the type of list that each participant will be given – this is your **independent variable**.

You would then need to consider how you were going to get any sort of results. Well, it would make sense for participants to look at the lists and then try to remember the words, and you could then compare which list produced the highest level of recall. The results of these memory tests would be your **dependent variable**.

Extraneous variables

You will need to consider if there are any additional variables (or extraneous variables, see page 250) besides the different lists, which might influence the results. Questions you need to consider are:

● Do the participants get the same instructions?
● Are they all 'performing' in the same place?
● Are the noise levels the same?
● Is the temperature the same for both groups?
● Are some of the participants usually much better than others at remembering word lists?

KEY CONCEPTS

The OCR examination requires candidates to be able to:

* frame a null hypothesis
* frame an alternate (research) hypothesis
* distinguish between null hypotheses and alternate hypotheses.

The hypothesis

If you decide that the organised list will be easier to remember, you are making a prediction based on an educated guess or a hunch. This prediction is known as a hypothesis. Your prediction is that the style of the list (organised or unorganised) will have an effect on recall (the number of words we are able to recall). This prediction follows a particular pattern for an experiment – that by manipulating one thing (type of list), it will have an effect on something else (number of words remembered).

The prediction is that participants who see the list of organised words will remember more words than participants who see the same words listed in random order. This is known as the **alternate or research hypothesis**.

What happens if you do get the results you predicted but (unbeknown to you) the results are not due to the organisation of the lists, but are just due to chance?

Perhaps it would be helpful (and safer) to test things the other way round as well. You could do this by also predicting that the difference in the number of words recalled is *not* due to the organisation of the lists, but is simply due to chance events. This is known as a **null hypothesis**.

This allows you to accept either your alternate hypothesis or your research hypothesis.

Alternate or research hypothesis	Null hypothesis
Participants who see the list of organised words will remember more words than participants who see the same words listed in random order.	Any difference in the number of words recalled by participants is *not* due to the organisation of the lists, but is simply due to chance events.

You can frame alternate and null hypotheses for any type of research. Below are some more examples.

Alternate or research hypothesis	Null hypothesis
Children who watch violent videos will hit a Bobo doll more often than children who have not watched violent videos.	Any difference in the number of times children hit a Bobo doll is not due to the nature of the videos they have watched, but is due to chance
When given a choice of seating, males are more likely to sit next to another person, but females are more likely to sit opposite another person.	Males and females, when given free choice of where to sit, will not have any preference for sitting either opposite or next to another person, and any seating preference that is observed will be due to chance.
There will be a correlation between the number of people in a group and the likelihood that individuals will conform to group norms, with a large group producing higher levels of conformity.	There will be no correlation between the number of people in a group and the level of conformity shown by an individual, and any correlation observed will be due to chance.

Design

When you know what you want to investigate, you will need to consider the design of your research; this will take into account the nature of the participants and what you want them to do. Perhaps they are very different from each other and this might be an issue if you have decided that you need two groups of people. Therefore you need to think how best to manage them (see Chapter 6, page 252).

- Should you use a repeated-measures design?
- Should you use a matched-pairs design?
- Should you use independent-groups design?

In our example, we could use any of these three methods. We could have two groups of participants who are matched for age (age affects memory) and ability (some people with learning difficulties have memory-related problems). We could just have a very large number of participants who are randomly divided and therefore any differences between the groups would be balanced out. We could actually use the same participants for both conditions but the problem then would be that they would be able to remember the words the second time around, which would make it easier for them. There are other ways of managing this, such as having two different lists (but you would have to make sure they were 'equal' in difficulty, which would be difficult).

KEY CONCEPTS

The OCR examination requires candidates to be able to:

- distinguish between a target population and a sample
- distinguish between random sampling and opportunity sampling
- describe the relative strengths and weaknesses of random and opportunity sampling, with reference to representative samples and biased samples.

Sampling

When conducting research, it is important to consider who the participants are likely to be. Obviously, your selected participants, or **sample**, must be representative of the population you are interested in researching, known as your **target population**. For example, if you are looking at the effects of age on memory, you would not want to simply consider teenagers. Your target population could be quite specific, such as six-year-olds, male adults, people sitting alone, insecurely attached children or heart attack victims, or it could be simply a range of people from all walks of life. If your sample represents the target population, you can generalise your results to the people in that target population.

Psychologists decide on the size of their sample by taking account of factors such as the experimental design (independent measures require more participants than repeated measures) and time available (a small sample is usual in an observational study because such a study is time-consuming and no hypothesis is being tested). Remember that, although a larger sample is often thought to be more desirable, it might not be more representative.

Once the numbers and characteristics of the participants have been decided, and any concerns about participant variables have been addressed, they can be selected using one of the three sampling methods described below.

Random sampling

Be warned, this is not what you think it is – random sampling is highly controlled! It means that every member of the target population has an equal chance of being selected. For instance, in a study with a target population of pregnant women, the names of all pregnant women across the country would be gathered. As each woman must have an equal chance of being selected, all their names could be written on a slip of paper and put in a box. To select 20 participants, the first 20 names taken out of the box would comprise the sample. Alternatively, every woman might be given a number and the participants could be selected using a random number table, an example of which is shown in Figure 6.1. To do this, start at any point in the table and move through it either horizontally or vertically. Stop at each number: the woman who has this number becomes a participant. When 20 participants have been selected, they are the sample.

03 47 43 73 86	39 96 47 36 61	46 98 63 71 62	33 26 16 80 45	60 11 14 10 95
97 74 24 67 62	42 81 14 57 20	42 53 32 37 32	27 07 36 07 51	24 51 79 69 73
16 76 62 27 66	56 50 26 71 07	32 90 79 78 53	13 55 38 58 59	88 97 54 14 10
12 56 85 99 26	96 96 68 27 31	05 03 72 93 15	57 12 10 14 21	88 26 49 81 76
55 59 56 35 64	38 54 82 46 22	31 62 43 09 90	06 18 44 32 53	22 83 01 30 30
16 22 77 94 39	49 54 43 54 82	17 37 93 23 78	87 35 20 96 43	84 26 34 91 64
84 42 17 53 31	57 24 55 06 88	77 04 74 47 67	21 76 33 50 25	83 92 12 06 76
63 01 63 78 59	16 95 55 67 19	98 10 50 71 75	12 86 73 58 07	44 39 52 38 79
33 21 12 34 29	78 64 56 07 82	52 42 07 44 38	15 51 00 13 42	99 66 02 79 54
57 60 86 32 44	09 47 27 96 54	49 17 46 09 62	90 52 84 77 27	08 02 73 43 28
18 18 07 92 46	44 17 16 58 09	79 83 86 16 62	06 76 50 03 10	55 23 64 05 05
26 62 38 97 75	84 16 07 44 99	83 11 46 32 24	20 14 85 88 45	10 93 72 88 71
23 42 40 64 74	82 97 77 77 81	07 45 32 14 08	32 98 94 07 72	93 85 79 10 75
52 36 28 19 95	50 92 26 11 97	00 56 76 31 38	80 22 02 53 53	86 60 42 04 53
37 85 94 35 12	83 39 50 08 30	42 34 07 96 88	54 42 06 87 98	35 85 29 48 38
70 29 17 12 13	40 33 20 38 26	13 89 51 03 74	17 76 37 13 04	07 74 21 19 20
56 62 18 37 35	96 83 50 87 75	97 12 25 93 47	70 33 24 03 54	97 77 46 44 80
99 49 57 22 77	88 42 95 45 72	16 64 36 16 00	04 43 18 66 79	94 77 24 21 90
16 08 15 04 72	33 27 14 34 90	45 59 34 68 49	12 72 07 34 45	99 27 72 95 14
31 16 93 32 43	50 27 89 87 19	20 15 37 00 49	52 58 66 60 44	38 68 88 11 80

Figure 6.1 Extract from random number tables

Advantages

This method of selecting participants *probably* provides one of the most representative samples you can choose, and you are more likely to get a greater variety of participants than you would by using some of the other methods that psychologists use. The results can therefore be generalised to the target population with more confidence, so a large sample is not necessary.

Disadvantages

This method can be time consuming; people may not agree to take part once they have been selected; you cannot use random sampling in some types of research, such as field experiments or questionnaires. Another disadvantage is that a random sample can be very unrepresentative because that is what can happen when we do things truly randomly.

Opportunity sampling

Researchers use opportunity sampling because it is quick and cheap in comparison with other methods. Anyone who is available and agrees to take part in the research can become a participant. Selecting names from a telephone directory is another example of opportunity sampling. This is not a representative sample, however, because many people who have phones are not listed in a directory and some other people do not have phones.

Advantages

It is easy and fast; it is used in natural and field experiments.

Disadvantages

The sample is unlikely to be representative; people may be asked to take part simply because they look approachable and cooperative. In order to increase representativeness, a large sample is necessary.

Self-selected sampling

A self-selected sample is one where participants choose to take part – for example, people who return questionnaires or who have volunteered to take part in a study (by responding to advertisements in newspapers or on the radio).

Advantages

People offering to take part are less likely to drop out; surveys enable you to have a large sample; they are easier and cheaper to conduct because you do not have to go through a selection process.

Disadvantages

A self-selected sample is extremely unlikely to be representative of the population as a whole; they are likely to be people who have more time, they may be more outspoken, have strong feelings about the topic you are researching, and so on; as the sample may be biased, results will be biased, so they cannot be generalised to the population as a whole.

Materials

Materials, equipment or apparatus used, such as a tape recorder, selection of photographs or word lists, need to be accurately

Model – someone whose behaviour is copied by another person

Nature – based on innate characteristics

Negative correlation – a relationship between two variables in which as one increases the other decreases

Negative reinforcement – anything which strengthens behaviour because it stops an unpleasant experience

Neuroticism – neurotics show traits of instability, tend to be very anxious, depressed, feel guilty, can be irrational, moody and emotional

Nonfamilial adoptions – adoptions by strangers rather than by family members

Nurture – when our experiences and upbringing are used to explain the way we think and behave

Obedience – following a command, order or instruction which is given by an authority figure

Object permanence – a child's understanding that although it can no longer see an object, the object still exists

Observational learning – human learning which takes place by observing others (social learning)

Observational method – research which involves watching and recording behaviour

Oedipus conflict – the conflict created by a boy's feelings towards his mother

Operant conditioning – learning which occurs as a result of reinforcement or punishment

Opportunity sampling – selecting whomever is available to be a participant

Participant variables – ways in which individual participants differ from each other, which may affect results

Perception – the process of interpreting, organising and elaborating on sensory information

Phobia – an intense, persistent and irrational fear of something which is accompanied by a compelling desire to avoid it

Physiological – related to the processes of the body

Positive correlation – a relationship between two variables in which as one increases the other increases

Positive reinforcement – anything which strengthens behaviour because it is rewarding

Practice effect – when participants do better on a task the second time they do it; it occurs in a repeated-measures design of study

Prejudice – an attitude towards a group, or a member of the group based on characteristics which are assumed to be common to all members of the group

Pre-operational stage – the second stage of cognitive development

Primacy effect – when you remember the first pieces of information you are given

Prototype – a prototype is an original type, or form, or instance of something which serves as a typical example. Prototypical is something which is very like the prototype

Psychoanalytic theory – a theory based on the idea that behaviour is caused by unconscious forces

Psychosexual – to do with the mental and emotional feelings about sexuality

Psychoticism – people with this trait are aggressive, cold, egocentric, are often impulsive and show no empathy for others

Puberty – the word puberty literally means to be covered in fine hair – and is derived from the Latin word 'pubescere', meaning to grow hairy or mossy. It is the period of time when a child becomes physically mature enough to be able to produce offspring

Punishment – anything that weakens

behaviour or makes a behaviour less likely to happen

Random sampling – selecting participants on the basis that all members of the target population have an equal chance of being selected

Range – the difference between the highest and lowest scores

Recall – searching the memory to retrieve some information previously learned

Recency effect – when you remember the last pieces of information you are given

Recognition – recognising something we have seen or learned before

Rehearsal – repeating information so that it is retained in memory

Reinforcement – anything that strengthens behaviour

Repeated measures – a design of experiment in which the same participants are in the control and the experimental group

Replicated – repeated

Response – the behaviour that results from a stimulus

Sampling – the method by which participants are selected for research

Scaffolding – Vygotsky said that with help and guidance (or scaffolding), a child would be able to demonstrate a greater ability than they could without the support and guidance from an adult

Scattergram – a way of showing the degree to which data is related

Schema – a 'packet' of information stored in our memories, which contains all we have learned about different things (such as objects or situations). Schemas can expand as we learn more about the world we live it

Self-selected sample – a sample comprising participants who choose to take part in research

Semantic information – the meaning of something

Semantic processing – processing something for meaning

Sensori-motor stage – the first stage of cognitive development

Separation distress – the unhappy response shown by a child when an attached figure leaves

Serotonin – a brain chemical or neurotransmitter which carries the electrochemical messages from one brain cell to the next

Sex identity – the biological status of being male or female

Sexism – discriminating against someone on the basis of their sex

Social categorisation – classifying people as members of a social group

Social context – what sort of social situation you find yourself in, for example in school or at the doctors

Social desirability – something that we find appealing in a social way. Some traits, such as friendliness, are very socially desirable whilst others are not

Social identity theory – the sense of who we are which is gained from membership of a group

Social learning – human learning which takes place by observing others; observational learning

Sociocultural approach – the impact of social interactions and cultural influences on something, for example the sociocultural approach to child development stresses the importance of social interactions with other people and the pressures from the culture in which a child lives

Standardised instructions – the identical instructions given to each participant in a study